Phoenix
in a
Bottle

*How We Overcame Alcoholism,
and are Able to Drink
Responsibly Again.*

Lilian and Murdoch
MacDonald

Published by:

MELROSE BOOKS

An Imprint of Melrose Press
St Thomas Place, Ely
Cambridgeshire
CB7 4GG, UK

www.melrosebooks.com

Second Edition © 2009

The Authors assert their moral right to
be identified as the authors of this work

Cover design by Bryan Carpenter

ISBN 978 1 907040 26 9

Printed and bound in Great Britain by:

CPI Antony Rowe. Chippenham, Wiltshire

FSC

Mixed Sources
Product group from well-managed
forests and other controlled sources

Cert no. SGS-COC-2953
www.fsc.org
© 1996 Forest Stewardship Council

The Legend of the Phoenix

Phoenix. A mythical bird, of gorgeous plumage, fabled to be the only one of its kind, and to live five or six hundred years in the Arabian desert, after which it burnt itself to ashes on a funeral pile, and emerged from its ashes with renewed youth, to live through another cycle of years.

Oxford Dictionary

The Phoenix bird symbolizes immortality, resurrection and life after death. In ancient Greek and Egyptian mythology it is associated with the sun god.

According to the Greeks, the bird lives in Arabia, near a cool well. Every morning at dawn, the sun god would stop his chariot to listen to the bird sing a beautiful song while it bathed in the well. Only one phoenix exists at one time.

When the bird felt its death was near, every 500 to 1461 years it would build a nest of aromatic wood and set it on fire. The bird was then consumed by the flames.

A new phoenix sprang forth from the pyre. It embalmed the ashes of its predecessor in an egg of myrrh and flew with it to Heliopolis, 'City of the Sun', where the egg was deposited on the altar of the sun god.

Contents

Preface

THERE is throughout the world a widespread mistaken belief that 'once an alcoholic, always an alcoholic', and that an alcoholic can never safely drink again. This fallacy is commonly believed by alcoholics themselves, and is perpetuated and promulgated by their own self-help organisation, *Alcoholics Anonymous*, of which we ourselves, both separately before we met, and together afterwards, were reluctant on/off members for many years. The *AA* line is followed in the main by the medical and psychiatric professions, and also by the vast majority of (but not all) alcohol treatment and counselling services.

So we have a situation today where *AA* has ring-fenced the territory of alcohol recovery, and its flawed ideas and theories about the necessity of lifelong sobriety are widely accepted throughout the world.

Lifelong sobriety is not recovery from alcoholism, as *AA* would have us believe. That is treating the symptom rather than the underlying cause, and is therefore just a damage-limitation exercise.

Merely staying sober, and going on the *AA* programme of 'recovery' means that they have arrested the outward problem of their self-harming behaviour, which is admirable. But they have failed to address the underlying psychological reasons why they were behaving like that in the first place. If they did that, then there is no reason why most of them would then not be able to drink responsibly again and behave themselves like everybody else.

AA disempowers people by making them accept the first of the Twelve Steps, which states: 'We admitted we were powerless over alcohol.'
We believe the opposite.

Nobody is powerless over alcohol. In fact nobody is powerless to change any aspect of their behaviour about which they are unhappy.

If you believe in people – and tell them that you believe in them – then they are capable of almost anything. And that is one of the main purposes of this book – to empower people to take control of their own lives, as we have done ourselves.

Back in 1994 my husband Murdoch and I were generally regarded as hopeless alcoholics. Local doctors and, more importantly, our own families had given up on us as we staggered from one alcoholic bender to the next. We seemed to have no future.

Today we have successfully overcome our problems, and have managed to get our lives back in order. We have a comfortable home, from which Murdoch runs his own PR business. Unusually, we are also able to drink safely again if and when we so wish. And, along the way, I have also overcome an eating disorder.

The purpose of this book is to offer hope to people with similar problems, not to mention their families, friends, employers and society in general.

The abuse of alcohol certainly caused the two of us major social problems, to the extent of finding ourselves homeless and practically down and out, not to mention nearly dying. It was obvious to us that something somewhere had gone terribly wrong in our lives – we decided to find out what. We went back to the beginning, and if like us, other alcoholics are willing to address their own issues from the past, they will come to their own understanding. They can radically change their lives, beholden to nobody but themselves, and become the master of their own fate instead of the slave.

In this book we tell our story – often harrowing, but also comical – which we believe will be of help not only to sufferers from the disorder which blighted more than half of our expected lifetime, but also to those with bulimia, anorexia and other so-called addictions conventionally treated with the *12-Step Programme*, which we believe are all branches of the same tree, with its roots in childhood.

I have described how we achieved this, not suggesting that this is necessarily the path that everyone must follow, but just to show that there is a way, and one that has certainly worked for us.

The opening chapters describe how things were at our lowest point. This is to prove that we were really alcoholics, because the standard response of *AA* when they are told that someone has recovered from alcoholism and drinking responsibly again is to say: 'Well, they were obviously not really alcoholics in the first place.'

Whether or not Murdoch and I were really alcoholics, we leave you, the reader, to be the judge.

Chapter One
Down and Out in Cambridge
1994

We shall not cease from exploration
And the end of all our exploring
Will be to arrive where we started
And know the place for the first time.
Through the unknown, remembered gate
When the last of earth left to discover
Is that which was the beginning;

T. S. Eliot, **Four Quartets**

WE both woke up simultaneously, as we invariably did when we were bender drinking, and peered around us. We were still on Christ's Pieces, a large open green behind the bus station in the centre of Cambridge. The sunny early October day, with the trees still leafy-green against a clear blue sky, had ended whilst we slept. All around was darkness, and we could barely see the outlines of the shrubs and bushes amongst which we lay.

Although the days that autumn had been warm, the nights were getting bitter, with a touch of ground frost just before dawn. We shivered as we struggled to our feet, deeply chilled in spite of the duvet in which we had wrapped ourselves – provided by one of our drinking companions earlier in the day, and stolen specially for us (we were proudly informed) from Marks & Spencer. It was already quite damp, as a fine light drizzle had started to fall while we had lain unconscious, and this was probably what had woken us.

1

But it wasn't just the cold and rain that made us shiver. Only another alcoholic can know the sheer terror of wakening up in the middle, or at the end of, a bender. Especially if it is night-time, and, worst of all, to discover (as we now did) that there is nothing left to drink, and no more money with which to buy any further supplies.

When we had fallen asleep there had been three-quarters of a bottle of gin left, which we had carefully concealed in between the two of us, and about £30 in our pockets, but now everything was gone, and the reason for the sudden disappearance of our erstwhile companions became apparent. We'd been robbed! When there's booze enough to go round, there's a certain easy-going camaraderie between alcoholics, but when booze and money run short, then it's dog eat dog.

Without even needing to tell each other, we both knew that we desperately needed a drink. Although there was almost certainly no money left in the bank, (we had made a last withdrawal early the previous morning), we decided as a last resort to try our cashline card one final time. Having hidden the duvet under a convenient bush, in case we needed it again, and gripping each other tightly by the hand, we made our way, step by weary step, back across the green, and into Drummer Street bus station.

After the silent darkness on Christ's Pieces, the glaring lights and the noisy hurly-burly of the town came as a sudden shock. But even worse was to follow. From behind us came a crowd of youths on the rampage. Seizing the lapels of my long coat and Murdoch's jacket they ripped them apart, roughly searching for money that they needed (so they shouted in our faces) for drugs. Eventually they realised that we were telling the truth when we said that we did not have any, that we had already been robbed that night, and they left us, lying on the ground, our clothes in tatters, and with me sporting a black eye. Even more wearily than before, and now painfully as well, we made our way out into St Andrew's Street, left up Petty Cury, and so to Market Square.

The illuminated clock-face over the Guildhall showed ten minutes to one, but as it was Friday night (or Saturday morning rather) there was no shortage of revellers thronging the square, weaving their way through the abandoned skeletons of the market stalls. Partly because of the paranoid fears of the alcoholic, partly due to the shame of our appearance (as well as my coat and Murdoch's jacket in shreds, my shoes were burst, Murdoch had a two-week growth of beard, and we were both filthy dirty from sleeping rough), we tried to avoid the crowds. I found a space to sit on a public bench at the front of the Guildhall, next to what appeared to be an old tramp silently sleeping, wrapped in an old dirty blanket, while Murdoch went on what proved to be an unsuccessful trip to the bank in Trinity Street to try our cashline card one last time.

We were both getting colder and colder, and the crowds in the square were beginning to thin out. The tramp on the bench beside us began to stir himself awake, and when we saw his face, we realised to our surprise that he wasn't an old man at all, but probably in his late twenties or early thirties. He told us that he hadn't had a drink for a couple of days – not only did he not have any money either, but he was also suffering from alcoholic paralysis, and could not move from the bench. We asked him for a loan of his blanket, and jokingly pointed out that we could take it from him if he didn't agree. He looked at us sadly and said, "But you wouldn't do that to one of your own, would you?" That made us think, and we left him alone after that. He soon fell back into a deep sleep, and we pulled the blanket a bit closer round him.

By this time we were close to despair. We were freezing, the alcoholic shakes were starting to seriously manifest themselves, and an awful dread was setting in as we realised that we could think of no possible way out of the mess that we were in, at least until the Monday morning, when we might be able to wring a last few pounds out of the bank. Before then, a whole weekend without anything to drink, nothing to eat, sleeping rough and perishing cold – we couldn't face the thought of walking back to Christ's Pieces for the duvet, even if we had been able to find it again.

I looked at Murdoch, his head sunk in his hands, rocking back and forwards with his elbows on his knees. I heard him whispering to himself the words of Jesus's despair as he hung on the cross: "Eloi, Eloi, lama sabachtani. My God, my God, why hast thou forsaken me?"

I said to him, "What are we going to do now, chuck?"

"I don't know, darling," he replied, "I just don't know."

I looked down and noticed that my legs had swollen to twice their normal size, my feet ached (I didn't know then that I had peripheral neuritis), and could hardly have put one foot in front of the other. The shame and sadness of my life came running through my head, and just sat staring into what seemed to be an empty black hole. I thought then that we were both about to die, and I told Murdoch so. We said what we thought were to be our last goodbyes, and then just sat there silently, holding on tightly to each other.

It had not been my first bender, and it was to prove, after all, not to be my last, but I will always think of it as my worst. I was in a strange city, I knew nobody, and when you get as low as that, somehow inevitably you yearn for your roots.

I wanted to go home, but I didn't know where home was. I had never seemed able to live the way I wanted to live. I felt separated from my true self – the person I really was, but had never been able to reach.

I must have fallen asleep for a minute or two, but I was suddenly awakened again. "Hello," I heard a voice say, "Are you all right?"

I looked up, and saw two girls, probably in their mid to late twenties, standing in front of us. The first was the one who had spoken to me, the other was taking Murdoch's hands away from his face, and asking him what the matter was.

They told us that they were both nurses at Cambridge's Adden-brooke's Hospital, that they had been out for a night on the town, and had just come out of a nearby disco. They had hardly any money left between them, but with it they insisted upon going across to a nearby

4

late-night stall in Market Square that was just on the point of closing, and buying a hamburger and a cup of tea for us to share between us.

Gradually, without meaning to, we found ourselves telling them the whole sad story. How, two months before, we had left our home in Scotland, and come to Cambridge (where Murdoch had spent his undergraduate years at university,) with the idea that he should now do research and take a PhD degree. How we had taken accommodation, and then been evicted from it when we had started this latest two-week bender.

Illegally evicted, as it turned out. The trouble was that we had been too honest for our own good, and had told the landlady that we were alcoholics at the outset, with the result that as soon as we first started drinking she feared for the worst, and put us straight out on the street. If we had had the sense to go straight to the Housing Department, a solicitor or the Citizens' Advice Bureau things might have been sorted out, since she still had two weeks rent in hand, and had refused to let us back in her house, even to get a change of clothing. But we were drinking, so we didn't bother. We just left quietly, and went and found ourselves bed and breakfast for the night. And carried on drinking.

The two nurses were listening intently to our story, one sitting on the armrest of the bench, the other kneeling in front of us.

It was about four o'clock in the afternoon when we booked our first night's bed and breakfast. We were asked to pay in advance, but that was no problem, as we still at that time had some savings left, and we had already been down to the bank to draw a good bit of it out. From the bank we had gone to the off-licence and bought a litre of gin, and rolled it in a copy of that day's *Cambridge Evening News*, together with a bottle of lemonade placed on top, a couple of bars of chocolate and some crisps and plenty of cigarettes. We felt like a couple of swells as we set off for the B&B, and didn't dream that any one there could possibly suspect how much we had been drinking, and that we were in the throes of a bender!

Having got through the registration formalities as quickly as possible, we shut our room door with a sigh of relief, opened the gin and took a long welcome draught. We also wolfed the chocolate and crisps, but don't forget that we hadn't eaten at all during the previous three days. A couple of large drinks later, and we were dead to the world.

I was awakened by Murdoch shaking my arm.

"Psst! Hey waken up, Lilian! Have you hidden the gin? I can't find it!"

At that I soon came round, pulled myself up, and, leaning on my elbows, took a quick scan round the room, and then I remembered - I had put it under my pillow 'for safety'!

I smiled at Murdoch, and said, "Nae bugger was going to get that while I was asleep!"

We had a couple of quick drinks, by which time it was getting on for seven o'clock in the evening. We decided to leave the rest of the bottle for the morning, go out and get another at the off-licence opposite, and take it down by the River Cam off Chesterton Road, overlooking Jesus Green on the other side.

It was a beautiful evening, and we sat for two or three hours chatting and laughing as if we hadn't a care in the world. There were some people on one of the houseboats, but apart from that, we had the place to ourselves. It was the last short time of peace and calm, illusory as it was, that we were to know for some considerable time.

We must have got back to our digs all right, because that is where we were wakened by the sound of the breakfast gong at eight o'clock. We could not face going into the dining room, but just sat on the bed finishing off the booze we had left for the morning. By now we both felt steady enough to take a shower, which was *en suite*, but this turned out not to be a good idea, as it was no bigger than a broom cupboard. I got in and could not get out, and Murdoch was outside and could not get in. By now we were both getting claustrophobic so we pulled our clothes back on and made for the exit as fast as we could.

The relief to get out into the fresh air settled us a little, but the rest of that day is just a blank. When we came to our senses it was late evening. I remember asking a passer-by where we were, what time and what day it was. Apparently we were on Midsummer Common and it was nearly half past eleven at night. By the time we got our bearings we were in St. Andrew's Street, desperate for a drink. All the off-licences were closed, and it was too late to find a bed and breakfast.

But then we saw the lights of a hotel in the distance, which turned out to be a Holiday Inn. We knew that if we could get in and take a room, then we would be able to get a bottle from room service, and although it would use up all the rest of our money, it would be worth it. In fact, in view of the state we were in, there was no choice. Murdoch had a comb in his pocket, with which we did our best to tidy ourselves up, then took two deep breaths and marched in as though we owned the place.

It paid off – all they asked for was the money up front, no questions asked. The first thing we did when we got into our room was order a bottle of gin, which duly came, on a silver tray with crystal glasses, lemon, ice and tonic water. We were in heaven again, but it was only momentary. After the excitement of seeing it there in front of us, we now had to pour it. My hands were shaking so much that I could not keep the bottle still. As much drink ended up on the tray as in our glasses, but eventually we managed it. All I remember after that was sitting on the end of the bed silently staring into space. I was in my own world now, and Murdoch in his, numbed by what was happening.

Morning came, and we felt worse now than ever. We never mentioned breakfast, but we had both each in turn shaken the empty bottle of gin, just to make sure that there wasn't the slightest drop left. We had slept in our clothes, so we were ready to leave. Murdoch went to reception to settle our account, and found that we had paid so much up front the night before, that we were actually due a refund. We took the money and ran. We were back on the streets again. We were back in our nightmare.

We walked back up Downing Street into St Andrew's Street, and decided to go into Emmanuel College and sit by the ornamental lake until it was time for the shops to open. There was an elderly gentleman standing by the edge of the water watching the ducks. We smiled a greeting from a distance, but avoided getting too close to him in case he realised the state we were in, and had us put out. Eventually he walked off in the direction of the college buildings, and we were left in peace.

There was a quiet serenity about the gardens. The only sounds we could hear were the gentle birdsong and the distant hum of the traffic. There was something soothing about being there that morning, it helped to calm us down a bit. But not for long. Remember, we were really seriously into a bender by that time, and on a bender there is only one priority for any alcoholic – the next drink.

Just as we were about to leave, a woman came running up to us carrying what turned out to be a bag of rolls to feed the ducks. She explained that she was late for work, and asked if we would feed them for her. We agreed, but as soon as she had gone we were overcome by hunger, and ate the rolls ourselves.

At last it was time for Sainsbury's to open. We hurried in, and I grabbed a basket as we headed for the wines and spirits shelves, got what we wanted and were making for the checkout, when all of a sudden a voice said: "I think that you have had enough already!" and an arm lifted the bottle out of our basket. I looked up and saw a youngish man, who must have been the store manager. He said that, if he sold us any more to drink to us in the state we were in, he would risk losing his licence. There was nothing we could do about it, but get out as quickly as we could.

We were not long in finding another place to buy what we wanted. I spotted a quiet lane where we could both have a good slug of gin each, before deciding what to do next.

The rest of the day was hazily spent on yet another of Cambridge's public greens, Parker's Piece. I do not remember anyone around us at all, although there must have been, I suppose. Eventually it was evening, the bottle now empty, as were the cans of lager that one of us must have bought sometime during the day. Double-checking them again, just to make sure that they were empty, we decided to stagger on in towards the town. Neither of us was able to sit still.

We had started to panic because it was getting cold and dark, and we had hardly any money left. There would be no staying at the Holiday Inn tonight! In fact it looked as if we might be sleeping rough, if we didn't think of something quickly. We made for the telephones at the main post office, and had the idea of ringing the Samaritans. We weren't suicidal, but we weren't a kick and a shout away from it.

We didn't know the number, and we wanted to keep what cash we had left, so we dialled the operator, and asked her to reverse the charges. Luckily the Samaritans accepted the call, and we were soon speaking to someone at the other end. Apparently their office was not too far away from where we were, so we arranged to go round there straightaway. Twenty minutes later we were at least out of the cold, sitting in a warm room in a comfortable chair, drinking a hot cup of coffee.

Our relief did not last long. The woman listened to our story most sympathetically, but at the end she started to look very embarrassed, and told us that there wasn't very much that she could do for us. What she meant was that there was nothing she could do for us! She patiently waited while we finished our coffees, and then pointedly told us that they were just closing, and that we would have to go. She got up, and politely showed us to the door. We were back on the street again.

But we didn't give up. We couldn't give up. It was getting later and later, and colder by the minute. The prospect of a whole night spent out in the open was getting ever more real, and ever more threatening. However, across the other side of Parker's Piece we saw the blue lamp outside the police station. Surely they would be able to help! Even the thought of a bunk in a cell behind bars didn't seem too awful now.

There was a silent queue of about six people waiting when we got inside. The desk sergeant seemed to deal patiently and interminably with each one, and our anxiety became more acute by the second. At last it was our turn, but as soon as we started telling our story yet again we got the same feeling that we had had back at the Samaritans – this person isn't interested, he doesn't care about us, we're only a couple of alcoholics after all.

Quietly the sergeant explained that this wasn't an accommodation agency, and that it wasn't really his job to find us a roof for the night, and, no, we couldn't have a bunk in one of his cells, not unless we cared to assault one of his officers, that is, or committed some other jailable offence. We thanked him politely, and took our leave. Back in the street again!

What were we going to do now? We were both starving and thirsty again, started to walk a bit further on till we came to the first pub. We stood in the light at the doorway and counted out our loose change. There were about two or three pounds, and by now we were down to rolling tobacco instead of cigarettes. We decided to go in and try to buy two pints of cider without drawing too much attention to ourselves. While Murdoch was at the bar I found a quiet corner table for us, where we could sit with our backs to the crowd. We both took a huge gulp from our drinks, and then tried to make the rest last as long as possible, while we took stock of our situation.

There now seemed nothing for it but to resign ourselves to spending the night out in the open. If only we could get something to eat first, and a good bit more to drink, to help us sleep, or at least to ease us through the long weary hours till morning!

Suddenly I had a brainwave. "Have you got the cheque-book?" I asked Murdoch. He put his hand into his jacket pocket and brought it out. "I don't think this will be much good," he said. "We haven't got a cheque card."

"We did have, but we must have lost it. Don't you remember?"

He looked perplexed – we've never had a cheque card!

"Right," I said. "Here's the idea. We find a restaurant that's still open, go in and have a bloody good feed, and as much to drink as we can manage in the time available, and then just pretend that we can't find our cheque card. The worst that can happen is we spend the night in chokey, but at least we'll be able to sleep, with luck!"

We finished our drinks and left, feeling a bit better than when we had gone in. We carried on down the main road, but unfortunately the first few restaurants we came to were closed for the night. Then, just as our newly found optimism was beginning to wane, we saw the lights of an Indian restaurant about a hundred yards ahead. And, if we had any doubts as to whether it was still open, they were soon dispelled by the tantalisingly aromatic smells that were soon wafting towards us. We stood outside for a few seconds as we went through our by now familiar warm-up routine – back straight, head up, shoulders back, deep breath, fingers crossed, "break a leg, darling!" and we're on! Cameras, lights, action!

I opened the door, looked round, and Murdoch was still standing there. "I don't think that this is a very good idea," he said.

"No, you're right," I said. "It's not a good idea. It's a *bloody* good idea! Come on – let's go and try!"

Inside, the restaurant was empty. The one lone waiter came towards us, smiling. He was fairly young, and I thought (did I imagine it?) that he looked a little suspiciously at us. However, with the benefit of hindsight, we may not have looked so bad as we felt at the time. I had a long shiny black and silver raincoat on that had been very expensive, was still fashionable, and, in spite of our escapades to date, would not have shown the dirt. One of my best silver shoes was split, and the sole was coming off, but already I had become adept at holding one foot in front of the other so that this sorry state of disrepair was not too apparent to others.

Murdoch looked the waiter straight in the eye, and asked for a table for two. That was the other advantage we had in our favour, Murdoch has a refined cultured voice, honed on the airwaves of the BBC, and this, coupled with my air of superiority, allowed us to get away with things with which we might not otherwise have been able to do.

We sat down, and were handed the menus and the wine list.

"Would you like something to drink while you are making up your mind?" asked the waiter.

"Two large brandies with ginger ale, please. Martell if you've got it. And two packets of Rothmans please." The words came rolling out almost without needing to think, and I added (under my breath) "Hurry up! Hurry up!"

The agony of the wait till he came back with our order was getting too much. I could not hold the menu steady, despite the fact that I had drunk that pint of cider earlier. The excitement of what we were doing had accelerated the shakes – it would take at least another double brandy to counteract this!

At last that messiah arrived with our order: cigarettes, booze – bliss! He enquired whether we had made up our mind about what we wanted to eat. To save time, we asked what he would suggest. He blethered on about some dish or other, but we were not really listening, and just smiled and agreed, and also told him to surprise us with a nice starter. As for wine, we ordered a bottle of hock and another of claret. Satisfied, he shut his note-pad, and leaned over to light the candle. By the time he had done this, our glasses were empty, and we asked if we could have two more large brandies while we were waiting.

I don't remember what the food was that night. I just know that we ate as much as we could, firstly because we knew that we would be glad of it during the long night ahead, and, secondly, because the longer we continued eating, the longer we could carry on drinking, and sitting in the warmth and comfort of the restaurant.

But all good things come to an end. We could have willingly gone on sitting there all night, but the waiter was beginning to hover, indicating that he was ready to close up and go home. All the rest of the tables had been cleared and re-set for the next day. There was just one hurdle to overcome. He brought us the bill.

By this time, however, this was no longer the problem it might have been earlier. With a nonchalant flourish Murdoch brought out our chequebook and proceeded to make out a cheque for the requisite amount, plus a reasonably generous tip. He put this on the plate with the bill, and our cashline card on top, and waited to see what would happen.

It was a bit like lighting the blue touch-paper and waiting for the big bang. But if we had half expected sirens to start wailing and dozens of policemen to burst in and drag us off to prison, what actually happened was an anti-climax. The waiter came back, pursing his lips, and scrutinising our cashline card a little doubtfully.

"I don't think that this is a cheque guarantee card," he said uncertainly. One of Murdoch's hands flew to his pocket, the other to his brow. "Oh my God!" he exclaimed, "I must have picked up the wrong card! Look, will it be all right if we put our name and address on the back? There's no way the cheque is going to bounce, there's plenty of money in the account to meet this."

Our fate hung in the balance. But my appearance and Murdoch's voice must have swung it, plus the fact that it was late, the young man was tired and wanting to go home, and he was there on his own, as the manager was off-duty. Anyway, we got away with it. Deliberately trying not to rush, and so arouse suspicion, we gratefully headed for the door, and freedom! Although what sort of freedom it was to prove we had yet to find out...

We managed, although very slowly, to make our way back to Parker's Piece. We had noticed before that there was a pavilion back on the other side, and it would provide a bit of shelter for us. Although almost dead on arrival, we both slumped down together on one of the benches, and fell asleep till about five-thirty. The effects of the drink by this time were wearing off, and the cold and damp seeping in. Groggily we got ourselves to our feet. We did not have the energy to move, but neither could we be still. By now we could hear the early morning traffic moving in the background. We were both parched, but now we had no money to buy anything to drink, not even a can of lemonade from a newsagents which we passed, and which was just opening.

However, just then we were crossing a side street, and outside the front door of one of the houses there were standing two pint bottles of milk, just as if they were waiting for us. I looked at Murdoch, and he looked at me, and without a word being spoken we walked down the street, and, as we passed the house we each picked up a bottle, removed the top, and gulped the milk down all in one go. Then we replaced the bottles neatly back on the doorstep, and walked quickly back to the main road.

The ice-cool milk had given us momentary relief, but now it was time for a real drink, but how were we going to get one with no money? Out of the blue came inspiration – I thought of my daughter Elaine. Although she had been glad to see the back of me when we had set off for Cambridge, nevertheless we were still on fairly good terms, and kept in regular contact. In fact, I had been phoning her two or three times a week before this bender had started, and I suddenly realised that she would have guessed by now that we were drinking.

We talked it over, and decided she was our best chance of getting some money that day. I would telephone her and reverse charges at seven o'clock when she would be up getting ready to go to work. I would ask her to stop at the bank on her way to the station, and draw some money out of her account at the cash dispenser. She could put the cash in an envelope addressed to the Bank Manager who knew us all personally (or thought he did!) together with a note asking him to credit the cash to our account, and put it through the letterbox. We would then be able to draw the money out in Cambridge later that morning. But would she do it?

We headed for the telephone boxes outside Lion's Yard. I made the call. When she answered, I said: "Elaine, it's Mum."

"I know you've been drinking," she replied. "I can tell from your voice. What is it now?"

I told her our story, and asked her about the money. At first she said: "Indeed I will not!" But then I told her that we had stopped drinking, and we needed some money as a deposit for some new accommodation, and that we needed it that day. Finally she agreed to lend us a hundred pounds, so I read her over our account number, which I got from our cheque-book, and stressed that she should write a note to the bank manager asking him to make sure the money was credited to our account that day. Elaine said yes, she would, and put the phone down. She wasn't pleased, but I knew that she would do it for me.

We came out of Lion's Yard, and glanced at the clock in the Post Office. It was ten minutes past seven. More than two hours before we could possibly try to draw money from the bank! Luckily inspiration struck again. I thought that other alcoholics might be out at this time of the morning too, and, if so we might be able to cadge the odd drink. We desperately wanted to stop drinking, but, as others who have been in this position will readily understand, you cannot choose the time. For some reason, once you have started on a bender, you have to let it run its course. You cannot just stop voluntarily; you have to be beaten into the ground.

15

When we had first come to Cambridge (and been sober), we had noticed that drinkers congregated on Christ's Pieces, so we headed in that direction. The whole green was deserted – except for one lone figure sitting on a bench at the far end, reading a newspaper.

My eyesight suddenly sharpened. "Murdoch, that guy's drinking. Let's just go over and ask him straight out if we can have some of his drink. Tell him we'll pay him back in a couple of hours, when we get the money from the bank."

Murdoch seemed a bit reluctant, but I pulled him by the sleeve and said, "I can't wait two hours!" He agreed, and suddenly we were heading towards the distant figure with suddenly new-found vigour. Like Elaine, he wasn't keen at first. But then, as he afterwards explained, he felt that he couldn't refuse, on account of the state that he saw we were in. He told us that his name was Tony. He was drinking out of a large bottle of strong cider; another full bottle was standing unopened by his side. This he handed over, saying: "You look as if you need it more than I do at the moment!"

As we passed the bottle between us, and each took our first welcome slug of the day, the words in Shakespeare's ***King Lear*** must have come into Murdoch's mind, for he suddenly quoted: "For this relief, much thanks!"

The litre bottle should have kept us going for quite a while, but it was gone in twenty minutes or so – it hadn't really hit the spot. But by this time we had told Tony a little of our story, and I think that he believed us about cashing a cheque at the bank, and he went to a nearby licensed grocer and bought half-a-dozen cans of Carlsberg Special.

Soon after Tony returned, a friend of his, an Irishman in his sixties called Dennis, arrived, also carrying a supply of cans, and there was soon a party under way. There we were, four merry drinkers, our cares and worries momentarily forgotten, sitting in the early morning sunshine earnestly putting the world to rights.

So busy were we, drinking and talking, that we even forgot all about cashing our cheque for a while. Instead of us standing at the bank doors waiting anxiously for them to open, as we would otherwise have been doing, in fact it was nearly ten o'clock by the time that we tore ourselves away from the revelry, and hurried up Trinity Street to deal with the serious business of the day.

In the bank I sat down at one of the small desks to write out our cheque. It always reminds me a bit of being in a pew in church, and in fact this time I did offer up a short prayer that we would manage to get our money. After the cider and strong lager I was no longer completely sober, and the cheque I wrote out was pretty illegible, and my signature was just a scrawl. But the most difficult part was yet to come.

I marched up to the counter as if I was doing the bank a favour by giving them my custom, and presented our cheque to the cashier. She looked at me very suspiciously, but luckily there was a security screen between us, otherwise she could not fail to have been overcome by the alcohol fumes.

I explained that we did not have an arrangement to cash cheques at that branch, but that if she telephoned our bank manager in Ayr, he would sanction the withdrawal. She didn't look too pleased, but she went away round the back anyway.

At times like this, when you are getting more and more desperate for your next drink, everything seems to take three or four times as long as it does when you are sober. She seemed to be away for an eternity, and when she did return there was a further delay. Our bank manager had obviously received Elaine's letter with the money, and had said that it was all right to cash our cheque for £100, but we needed to give some form of identification.

We rummaged through our pockets and my handbag, and came up with our cashline card and my driving licence. She studied both of these at length, and at last, apparently failing to discover anything wrong with them, grudgingly started to count out the cash. Gratefully I snatched it up, and headed for the door.

The next, and most urgent, port of call was a public toilet. You have to be drinking like us, and living on the streets, to appreciate what a perennial problem this is. We came back down Trinity Street, crossed diagonally through Market Square, and walked down the side of *The Red Cow* to the conveniences at the rear entrance to the Lion's Yard shopping precinct. Having utilised the facilities, and purloined a toilet roll for use in future emergencies, we could now take a fresh breath, and concentrate on getting our next drink.

We had promised Tony and Dennis that we would be back, so we went to the off-licence in Market Square and bought cider and some cans of lager for them, and a large bottle of gin and some tonic for ourselves. As we were now back in the money again, we treated ourselves to some paper cups and a couple of packets of tailor-made cigarettes. Not only that, but on the way back to Christ's Pieces (or the green lounge, as we called it) we stopped and bought two large hot dogs with lashings of onions from a street vendor opposite Woolworth's. The smell had proved irresistible.

We got back to the green, gave back the bottle of cider and the cans of lager that we owed to Tony and Dennis (much I think to their surprise), and started into our own tipple. Although several more drinkers had joined the gathering, however, the light-hearted atmosphere of earlier that morning had dissipated. Everyone was beginning to get tetchy and quarrelsome. It had started to rain, and it seemed to be getting dark earlier than you would expect, as it often does on days like that in October. Gradually people started to drift away, and we were left on our own.

We were starting to get decidedly damp, so we made our way to the shelter of the bus station in Drummer Street, where we stopped for a couple more drinks. But although we were mixing ourselves strong ones, they were not having the desired effect. They were not numbing us from awareness of reality, and realisation of the awfulness of our situation was increasingly impinging upon our consciousness.

We decided we had to try to get hold of our belongings from our former accommodation – if nothing else we urgently needed a change of clothing – so we found another phone box and rang the landlady. She didn't want us back anywhere near her house, and we didn't want to admit that we were homeless, so we agreed to meet at the railway station, where she and her friend would bring our cases by car.

There were still a good couple of hours to go before the time that we had arranged to meet them. We decided to put these to good use, and find ourselves some accommodation for the night. We still had about £80 left, which would have been enough to pay for somewhere to stay, a warm bed, a chance to wash, and (of course) another bottle to see us through the night and plan our next move. But it was not to be.

We walked through the bus station out into Emmanuel Street, where we picked up a taxi. We asked the driver to help us find a bed and breakfast place that would take us in, and he took us to three or four in turn that he knew, but all of them pretended that they had no rooms available. We knew that this was not true, as they all had a 'Vacancies' sign in the window, and, anyway, the expression of disgust with which they looked us up and down was a dead give-away. I would have to admit that we must have presented a pretty awful picture, and I can't really blame them for turning us away. But now it was time to take the taxi to the railway station, and keep our appointment with our former landlady.

She was there with our cases when we arrived, and left them with us. So we were reunited with our belongings, but now had the problem of what to do with them. We had nowhere to go for the night, and we were in no fit state to carry four unbearably heavy suitcases around with us all night. Murdoch and I just looked at each other helplessly. The left luggage office was closed for the night, so we decided that we would just have to leave them where they were – we tried, but we couldn't even lift them between us. We reckoned that they would be safer there than anywhere, that they would be collected up in due course by the staff at the station, and we would be able to reclaim them sometime later when this nightmare was over.

"Right," I said to Murdoch, "we'll just have to head for the hills." So we did.

When we did go back to the railway station about a couple of weeks later to get our belongings back, we were informed by an irate stationmaster that, almost immediately after our hasty departure, our abandoned luggage had been noticed, the police and the bomb disposal squad had been called in, the station had been evacuated for three-quarters of an hour, and that we had single-handedly brought to a standstill every train in the whole of five counties.

At the time, however, we were blissfully unaware of all the chaos we had left behind us.

We fell into a taxi outside the station, and asked to be taken to the bottom of St Andrew's Street. Getting off there, we knew that by walking back towards the centre of town we would be certain of finding an off-licence on the way. Sure enough, Haddows was still open, and we went in to buy another litre of gin, some more tonic water and forty cigarettes. We still had some plastic cups left, so that even though we did not have a roof over our heads, at least we were sufficiently fortified to face the long night ahead.

By now we were both only just able to walk, and we shuffled wearily along, our backs stooped, hanging on tightly to each other like two very old and infirm pensioners. We retraced our steps of that morning, crossed back through Market Square, and went to sit down on the low wall outside King's College. Sometimes on a bender you instinctively feel the need to get into, or at least near to a church or other holy place. When the spirit is dying within, you thirst for some sort of comfort or consolation, some sort of vestige of hope, some sort of strength that you can no longer find within yourself.

We poured ourselves a large drink each, and smoked a long, contemplative cigarette. King's College Chapel behind, and Great St Mary's Church in front of us were both illuminated with an eerie light, and a quiet hush seemed to spread over Cambridge as the town settled down for the night. We felt as if we were the only ones condemned to stay out in the cold.

I said to Murdoch, "We must get back to *AA*. We must – anything is better than this."

"All right," he replied, "if that is what you want."

"No," I said. "It's not what I want. But there's no choice now. They are right and I've been wrong. At least you get a welcome there, nobody else seems to want us. Come on, let's go somewhere where there's a bit more shelter."

Wearily we gathered together our drinking and smoking requisites into a plastic carrier bag, and they started clinking against each other as we struggled to our feet. We were just passing the Senate House where Murdoch had received his degrees more than a quarter of a century before. I smiled at him ruefully, and said, "It wasn't always like this, was it? Never mind. We may be down, but we're not out yet!"

But just then, as we were passing the academic gown shop on the right, I suddenly felt as if I couldn't walk another step. There's another little old church there behind some railings, with a bench in front of it. Somehow or other, I struggled onto it, but could go no further. I felt as if I would never move from that place again. Murdoch sat down beside me, and I turned and looked at his once lovely face. It was now topped with a mass of unkempt hair, and sported nearly two weeks' growth of stubbly beard. There was a sore weeping on the side of his neck.

Inevitably, we poured ourselves another drink. By this time the alcohol was doing absolutely nothing for us, but the desperation, or rather the determination to carry on drinking was unabated. It was almost as if, unconsciously, we wanted to get the bender over as quickly as possible.

The feeling of alcoholic paralysis was spreading over my entire body, and sheer panic began to set in. Our voices were trembling with fear as we spoke to each other.

"You'll need to get me into hospital," I said. "I don't want to die out here in the street. And anyway I'm not really ready to go just yet."

Murdoch had to leave me to go and telephone for an ambulance, and he seemed to be away for ages. At least the streets were empty, and there was nobody around to witness our distress. At last he came back, and we made sure of one last drink and a cigarette before the ambulance arrived. We saw the blue flashing light reflected on the walls of the mediaeval buildings even before we heard the sound of its engine, but at least there was no siren blaring to disturb the silence of the sleeping city.

The paramedics were friendly, and asked me interminable questions while they took my pulse and blood pressure, and then started lifting me onto a stretcher. When they had strapped me in, they carried me into the ambulance, and then assisted Murdoch in behind me. Help was to hand at last! One paramedic drove, the other stayed in the back with us He was chatting away, but by this time, I was drifting into a deep sleep, and I don't remember anything more about the journey.

In fact, when I came round, I was lying in a cubicle in the Accident & Emergency Department of Addenbrooke's Hospital. A doctor had apparently just finished examining me, and was trying to get me to answer some questions. Most seemed to be about how long we had been drinking, and how much we drank. I answered as best I could, but my mind wasn't really focusing. I was really just wanting a warm dry bed, and I was praying that they would admit me, as this would have been our one hope of coming off this horrendous bender. But there was to be no reprieve that night.

"Well, there doesn't seem to be anything wrong with you, apart from the alcohol," he said. "You must stop drinking, and you must stop now. You can go as soon as you are ready."

I wanted to tell him that I wanted to stop, but couldn't, but what was the point? And anyway, I just didn't have the energy. I turned to Murdoch, who was sitting on the other side of the trolley that I was lying on, and whispered to him that I needed a drink. He whispered back that we couldn't drink there, but I told him that if he poured me one, I would take it into the toilet nearby and drink it. This we did, but just as I got back, the doctor passed the cubicle, looked in and said, "Oh good. You can walk again all right." Then he disappeared once more.

While Murdoch was taking his turn with his plastic cup of gin in the toilet, a nurse came in and said that we would have to leave now, as they needed the cubicle for another patient. Her tone implied that this other patient, or any other patient in fact, was far more needy and deserving of medical care and attention than I was. Murdoch returned with our plastic bag, and slowly we shuffled our way back to the main entrance. The clock by the door showed us it was now twenty minutes past one in the morning. In the middle of a bender, it often wasn't important what day it was, but knowing the exact time assumed a greater significance.

As we made our way back out to the main road, we realised that we were worse off now than ever. Now we were stuck here, a good three or four miles out of town, and with no means of getting back that night, short of phoning for a taxi. But what for? Instinctively, we wanted to save all the money we could. We had enough drink and cigarettes left to see us through the night, so we decided to find somewhere to get some sleep, and then set off back to town in the morning.

So that was how we ended up spending that night in a bus shelter outside Addenbrooke's Hospital. Luckily it had one long bench in it, not individual seats, so we managed to get a few hours' sleep. Occasionally we would wake briefly for a sip of gin, or a quick puff of a cigarette, but mostly we slept, or just dozed. The only interruption was just before dawn (the sky was beginning to shade from black to grey) when a passing police patrol car stopped somewhere near us. We were vaguely conscious of torchlight flashing across us, and of a voice saying: "Just leave them, they're not doing any harm."

We came to briefly then, and decided that we would start walking into town. But we must have fallen asleep again, to be wakened only by the sounds of people arriving at the bus shelter to queue up for the first bus. Hurriedly we gathered everything together and beat a hasty, not to mention embarrassed retreat. We needed a drink and a cigarette, but not in front of a crowd of curious commuters!

On the main road a signpost showed us the way back into Cambridge, and just about a hundred yards along there was a phone box, so we stopped off there for a quick refreshment and a smoke. Until the first slug, our heads had felt numb and befuddled, but as the first draught of alcohol slipped down our throats, something like full consciousness returned like a breath of fresh air, and we were soon fit enough to start our long slow shuffle back towards civilisation.

It must have been four or five miles, and we had to stop several times for a rest on the way. The time on the clock at the Catholic Church as we made our weary way back up Hills Road was ten minutes to nine, but the consolation for this was that the shops were open, and we could renew our supplies. We dumped the by now empty litre bottle of gin in a litter bin at the side of the road, and immediately replaced it with another from an off-licence that we came to. We went into the Lion Yard shopping arcade to get a bit of warmth, and sat there quietly sipping and smoking for the rest of the morning. We were desperately tired and weary, but we dared not fall asleep in case the police arrested us. Similarly, our drinking had to be disguised by wrapping a discarded newspaper around the gin bottle.

There was another drinker there that morning who wasn't quite so vigilant or discreet, and who subsequently paid the price.

When we first saw him he was recumbent outside a jeweller's shop near the spiral staircase. He was fast asleep and snoring stertorously. Neatly placed beside him was his bag of shopping, out of which protruded a long French baguette and a bottle of whisky.

A curious passing mongrel dog, not content with such uninteresting fare, decided to investigate further. Rummaging into the depths of the bag, he emerged, triumphantly clutching between his jaws a pound of best butcher's pork sausages. He trotted off, tail high and wagging delightedly, just as fast as his wee short legs would carry him. Unfortunately in his enthusiasm he had sent the bottle of whisky flying, and it now lay in several pieces, its amber contents spreading onto the marble tiled floor of the shopping mall.

Meanwhile, the unconscious drinker, blissfully unaware of the fate of his supper, was about to undergo a further unexpected indignity. A shopkeeper must have complained about his unwelcome presence, because just then two policemen marched up, and proceeded to wake him from his slumbers.

They were obviously intent on taking him away to sober up in a cell for an hour or two, but he was far less concerned about his imminent arrest and loss of liberty, than he was about the discovery of the destruction of his precious bottle of whisky, and the theft of his sausages. As he was led away, we heard him shouting: "It's not fair. You're arresting me, and the thieving bastard who stole my sausages and broke my bottle is going free! I might like the occasional drink, but I'm not a thief!"

Rather fearful after this encounter, we ventured outside to the back of Lion's Yard, where there are some seats around a courtyard. By now it was the afternoon, and a bit warmer. We sat down where it was quiet, and not too conspicuous, and we managed to doze off from time to time in the gentle autumn sunlight, but made sure we always remained upright in our seats in order not to attract any unwanted attention. Regularly sipping gin kept the worst of the panic away, but in its place a persistent numbing despair set in.

We no longer even thought of how we were going to get out of the mess that we were in – I suppose that we just assumed that we never would. We had enough money to keep us going for the time being, as we weren't eating or smoking much, and as for our drinking, we were just 'topping up' with occasional gentle sips. Even this was sometimes getting nauseous, but we had to continue. You can't just come off a bender voluntarily whenever you choose.

You get very restless on a bender, too – you can't seem to stay still in the same place for very long at a time, (except when you're sleeping), so as soon as we started waking up again, we both felt that we had to be moving on. We needed to buy another bottle anyway before the shops shut, to help to see us through the night.

Starting about that time, both our memories begin to get a bit hazy. Thereafter, neither of us can recall exactly complete days or whole nights. Instead all we have are random flashbacks and fragmented recollections. Neither of us is precisely certain where we slept that night, or even if we slept at all.

We both vaguely remember a vain attempt at normality, going into *The Red Cow*, and sitting in the lounge with a pint of cider each, watching *The News at Ten*, just as if we were a normal couple out for a quiet drink together after a hard day at work. Except that this particular couple had a litre of gin concealed beneath their seat, and this particular couple had no home of their own to go back to after they left the pub.

Much later one night (we're not sure whether it was the same one), we crept back into the Holiday Inn, and went upstairs and sat down in the lounge amidst the warmth and the soft background music. It gave us a momentary respite from the cold, but not for very long. There was a rather snooty couple at the next table, and I think that they must have complained to the management. Whatever the reason, we soon found ourselves being courteously but firmly escorted back down to into the street.

There were more bus shelters, there were more park benches (we could write a *Michelin Guide* to Cambridge, for dossers!) And, most of all, in spite of the increasing difficulty both of us were having in walking; there was a lot more aimless wandering around. Where it led us, most of the time we will never know.

In the early hours of one morning, however, I do know that we found ourselves standing in a queue on a stairway. We continued to stand for some considerable time, before it occurred to us to ask what we were queuing for. When someone kindly informed us that they were waiting to get into a late night disco called Sinbad's, we decided not to bother staying, and continued on our weary way.

We were barely conscious of days and nights passing, certainly not of how many did pass. We no longer knew what month it was, let alone what day, and once or twice we had to ask people in order to find out. But even at the end of a bender such as this, amidst the swirling fog of half memories, we did sometimes get a few hours, sometimes even half a day of sudden clarity.

Early one morning we awoke sitting quietly together on Christ's Pieces. For the time being, the dreadful burden of depression had been lifted from us, our paralysing fears had disappeared. There were even a couple of drinks each left in our bottle, with which to start the day, and some cigarettes as well. We felt almost happy again, and we decided we should have one last party, just the two of us, before reality returned.

We counted out the money, and there wasn't all that much. But we were not going to let a little thing like that stop us. We determined to phone the bank manager ourselves, and ask him for an overdraft. This time we had no fears about the outcome, and as so often happens when one is sufficiently confident, things worked out the way we planned. In fact, even better, because as well as authorising us to cash another cheque at the Trinity Street branch, he also agreed to pay the cheque we had issued to the Indian restaurant as well. But he had known me for many years, and my credit had always been good in the past.

Delighted with our morning's work, we quickly replenished our stores of gin and cigarettes, and set off back to the 'green lounge' again. Tony and Dennis were there already, drinking with some of their friends, and for a while we joined them, putting the world to rights again. It was a beautiful morning, and temporarily we seemed to have recovered some of our zest for drinking, and we were making swift inroads into our own bottle, as well as accepting the odd can of cider or super lager from our new-found friends. They asked us how we were getting on with our search for new accommodation, and we had to tell them that we still didn't have anywhere to stay. They wanted to know where we intended to sleep that night, and we replied that we would probably make do with the 'green lounge'. They seemed to have other plans for the morning, and drifted off after that, leaving Murdoch and me to our private party.

We refilled our glasses, drank each other's health, lit cigarettes and started to chat cheerfully as if there were no tomorrow. Around midday a very unfamiliar feeling crept over us – hunger! We realised that it must have been several days since we had last eaten, since we had last felt able to eat, in fact.

But now we thought we could definitely manage something, so we went and found a baker's shop-cum-restaurant on the corner of St Andrew's Street and the Drummer Street arcade. There we bought two of the most delicious piping hot sausage rolls either of us had ever tasted, as well as a couple of Chelsea buns, which we devoured ferociously on the way back to the green.

There the remains of the day passed quietly and pleasantly, and before we knew it, darkness started to fall. As it did so, a couple of our drinking companions returned, one of them struggling with a large box. It turned out to be a king-size duvet, which (he claimed) he had stolen especially for us from Marks & Spencer earlier that day. We thanked him profusely, and offered him a drink from our bottle, but were not too upset when he refused and took his leave, because by this time, although it was only early evening, we could hardly keep our eyes open any longer.

We unwrapped the duvet, dragged it into the midst of the bushes, laid it out flat, lay down in the centre of it with our bottle between us, tucked the sides in around us, and fell fast asleep…

I have already related how we awoke later that night, with the bottle and the remainder of our money stolen, and with no possible means of getting any more until at least after the weekend. Of how we were attacked while we were walking up to Market Square, and how we had finished up there, cold hungry and hopeless.

The two nurses could hardly believe our story, but unfortunately our tragic-looking appearance made it all too credible. Quickly they leapt into action, as if divinely inspired.

"Are you hungry?" asked one. "Would you like a cup of tea?" inquired the other. Together they opened their purses, and counted out their money between them. They told us they had been out for a night on the town, and it turned out that they had precious little cash left, but they insisted that we were welcome to what little they had. There was a hamburger stall in the square that was just on the point of closing, and they went and bought us a cup of tea each and a hamburger between us. Apart from the sausage rolls that morning, we had eaten practically nothing for several days, and were very hungry.

As we ate, and sipped our tea, the nurses immediately turned to other equally urgent practical matters – the question of where we were going to sleep that night. They were adamant that we could not spend it out in the open again, and we were all too willing to agree with that.

They said that they would go and find a phone box, and would ring the hospital and anywhere else they could think of in order to find out if there was a hostel or somewhere similar that would be willing to take us in. Meanwhile, we were put under strict instructions to stay exactly where we were, and not to move, as they would come back to us, whatever they did, or did not manage to find out for us.

They were away for ages, although it probably seemed longer than it actually was. There was not much temptation for us to move in fact, since we were paralysingly cold, and tired and weary. But equally, the effects of the alcohol were beginning to wear off, and the shakes were starting to set in. We felt the old familiar feeling of needing to move about, so, painfully slowly we shuffled off in the direction in which the nurses had gone.

And, in fact, we hadn't gone more than a few yards when we met them coming back. They seemed delighted with what they had managed to achieve, and when they told us, so were we. They had been told the name and address of a hostel that might be willing to take us in, but first there was the problem of how to get to it.

It wasn't that it was all that far. Soon (although we didn't know it then) we would be walking from there into the centre of town at least once every day. But that night we would never have made it, even if our lives depended upon it (and actually, they did).

But the resourcefulness of the nurses was not yet at an end. Glancing round the square, they spotted an elderly Scots reveller (why is the nationality of a Scots reveller always so blatantly obvious, even at a distance?). He was dancing his way lightfootedly between the market stalls, with an unopened bottle of champagne tucked under his arm, singing merrily, and inviting everybody he passed if they would join him in a 'Gay Gordons'. He was heading our way, and the nurses caught his attention and beckoned him over. Briefly they explained the situation, and asked him if he could possibly pay our taxi fare to the hostel, if they went away and ordered one.

The Scotsman took off his bonnet and scratched his head thoughtfully. "Och weel," he said, "I dinna ken aboot that!" But finally he agreed, and one of the nurses sped to the taxi rank outside the bus station, and soon came back with it. Before Murdoch and I even had time to properly say goodbye or thank any of our kind benefactors, the taxi was whisking us away to our last hope of warmth and shelter that night.

Our troubles weren't quite over yet, however. At first there was no reply when we rang the bell. Eventually a voice with a foreign accent came over the intercom, and in answer to our inquiry replied that they were full up. Then we started pleading, telling him how we had been attacked and robbed, and that we would be grateful to be allowed to sleep on the floor, if that was all there was available. At last the door was opened, and the night warden let us in. He looked a bit aghast at our appearance, and quickly started bustling around to get us somewhere to sleep.

He showed us into a kind of waiting room, and gave a couple of tugs at a settee standing against one of the walls, and instantly, as if by magic, it was transformed into a makeshift double bed, which, in our condition that night, looked like the ultimate in unimaginable luxury. Ermez (as he introduced himself to us) left us alone, while he hurried off to fetch covers and pillows, and finally bade us goodnight, explaining that we would have to see the day staff in the morning about staying any longer. Murdoch and I just sank into the bed in our clothes in sheer relief.

We only managed to doze fitfully and fretfully, as we were too anxious about what was going to happen the next day to be able to sleep properly. Holding on to each other tightly, afraid I was going to fall apart, I said to Murdoch, "Say that prayer that you know, and I will say it back to you." Murdoch started:

"Lord, keep us safe this night,
Secure from all our fears.
May angels guard us while we sleep,
Till morning light appears.
Amen."

More relaxed now, I was able to release my grip on Murdoch, and we managed a few hours of comparative peace and calm.

Chapter Two
Climbing Back Up in Cambridge

To dry one's eyes and laugh at a fall,
And baffled, get up and begin again.

Robert Browning, **Life in a Love**

ALL too soon we heard the sounds of the hostel beginning to come alive again. The doorbell rang several times in quick succession, and we presumed that it was the day staff arriving for duty. There were muted voices, one of them being that of Ermez, talking and occasionally laughing too. We wondered if they were talking about us.

We had a couple of cigarettes left each, and we smoked one of these now, passing it to and fro between us. At last, there was a knock at the door and a woman came in. She said good morning, told us her name was Julia, and asked us how we had slept, just as if we were on holiday, and staying at her hotel.

Then, without saying anything more, she went over to the window and opened it wide. We remembered how dirty we must have been, the alcohol fumes we must have been exhaling, and that considering also the cigarette smoke, the atmosphere in the room must have been rather pungent, to say the least.

Julia sat down on a chair by the window. She had obviously been fully briefed by Ermez, as she knew exactly how and why we had ended up there at the hostel. She had only one comment to make. "You two really have reached rock bottom. You need help with a capital H!"

In our case, help with a capital H began with a good hearty breakfast. It was being served at that moment in the hostel dining room, but my legs could hardly move, and anyway neither of us could have faced too many people in close proximity. Julia rose to the occasion, and came to our rescue. Disappearing for a few minutes, she returned carrying a huge tray full of hot steaming food, and a generous jug of freshly made coffee. There was a platter each of sausage, bacon, eggs, fried bread, mushrooms, tomatoes and black pudding – the works!

As she put the tray down on the table and invited us to tuck in, there was another knock at the door, and Julia was called away, saying she would be back in ten minutes. She was, and by that time there was not a scrap of food left on either of our plates, and the coffee jug was not so much empty as bone-dry. She seemed almost as pleased as she was surprised at the alacrity with which we had eaten, and went away and fetched more coffee for us all, and then we sat down and talked, while Murdoch and I treated ourselves to a whole cigarette each.

We told her how we had come down to Cambridge from Ayr in Scotland, planning for Murdoch to do research for a PhD degree. Going on this bender and losing our accommodation, not to mention all our money, had obviously put a damper on these plans, at least for the time being. What we needed now was a temporary refuge, to allow us to re-establish ourselves, and get our lives back into some sort of order. Most of all we needed time to think, not just about what we were going to do, whether we were going to carry out our original ideas and stay in Cambridge, or go back to Ayr and start again, but also how we were going to sort out the problem of our drinking.

Julia listened carefully. "This is Saturday," she said. "There's not a lot we can do until Monday morning, when Neville, the manager will be back in. But I've phoned him at home, and he says we can give you one of our bedsits just for the weekend. Then on Monday we'll put you through our admissions procedure, and see if we can keep you on longer term. I don't see why we shouldn't be able to. But if we can, you'll have to move back over here into the main block, and it'll be a case of two small single rooms until some bedsits become available, and until we know that you're going to be suitable."

So far as it went, we were delighted and grateful, and we said so. Julia smiled, but ever practical, said that she would show us to our room, and make arrangements for us to wash our clothes in the hostel laundry. That raised another problem – the only clothes we had were the ones we were standing in! Julia raised her eyes to high heaven. "Oh well," she said, "we'll see what we can do for you."

She took us to our room, which was in a block on the far side of quite a large, pleasant garden with trees and seats in it. She let us in through a security door, and, half way up the stairs she stopped and went into a walk-in cupboard. She sorted out some clothes for us, and we took them up to our room to try them on for size.

I put the bundle on the bed to see what we had. Luckily there was a pair of trousers and a jacket that fitted Murdoch perfectly, a couple of shirts that, when he rolled the sleeves up, looked fine. There were no ladies clothes at all, except for a quilted housecoat, but there were about four pairs of giant Y-fronts that would have fitted an elephant, and an enormous gent's vest. I tried the vest on and found that it came down to my knees, as did Murdoch's newly acquired underpants.

There was a large mirror in the room, in which we gazed at our two reflections. We turned to each other and burst out laughing hysterically. I had remembered one of the things Julia had said when she first saw us: "You two really have reached rock bottom!" When I repeated this to Murdoch, he turned to me and said, "Well, at least it's rocks we've hit, and not quicksands!"

He then finished dressing, whilst I settled for the housecoat, and we then shakily bundled all our dirty clothes into a black bin bag.

Julia herself came back at this point to show Murdoch where the laundry room was, and how to work the machines. Before they went, Murdoch told me that, while the clothes were washing, he would use the change from the taxi fare the previous night, and go and get us a packet of ten cigarettes, which would be all that we would have to last us the rest of the weekend. I waited in the room until he came back, as I was too shaky, and my legs were too weak for me to go with him, and besides, I was not really properly dressed.

When he returned our clothes were clean and sweet smelling. We could hardly put them on when we ourselves were still filthy dirty, so we went in search of the bathroom. But after the water had been running for only a few minutes, the panic attacks returned, and we were barely able to stay in the bath long enough to have a proper wash, but it was better than nothing. Julia had left us clean towels and talcum powder, so you can imagine that by this time we were already beginning to feel a lot better than when we had first arrived.

Lunch was being served in the main hostel building, but I still couldn't face going over, so Murdoch went and brought back (with great difficulty!) two plates of quiche and salad, and some fresh fruit. I could hear him coming long before he got to the door, as everything on the tray was jumping up and down and rattling like mad. He was feeling very shaky, but ate what he could, and gave the rest to me. I was ravenous, and scoffed everything in sight, and was still hungry. You can never tell, coming off a bender, sometimes you want to eat, but can't keep anything down, while at other times your stomach is like a bottomless pit. For me, this was one of those latter times!

There was a more substantial meal served in the evening, and menus were posted in advance outside the dining hall. Murdoch had had a look to see what there was in store for us later, and reported back that it was to be spaghetti bolognese. Perhaps to you reading this, that doesn't sound wildly exciting, but coming off that two-week bender, we were dreaming and drooling about that spaghetti all afternoon.

Julia had offered us an appointment with the hostel doctor, who would probably have prescribed us a ten-day decreasing dose course of valium or librium to alleviate the shakes, and to lessen the chances of our getting the DTs or hallucinations. But we had found in the past that for us sometimes the effect of these pills can be worse than going cold turkey, so we said thank you, but no thank you, we would sweat it out on our own.

Actually, that afternoon we didn't feel too bad – it was the lull after the storm. We had a temporary roof over our heads, and we were safe and warm for the weekend, at least. We decided that we would try to go out for a short walk in the early evening, just before dinner-time, even if it was just around the hostel garden, but until then I lay on the bed and Murdoch sat in the easy chair, and we began to talk about what we were going to do. Much as I hated the idea, I was beginning to think that we would have to seriously consider going back to *AA*.

When Murdoch and I had first got together (we actually met at an *AA* meeting at Green Street Lane in Ayr), we were both unhappy with the *AA* ideas and philosophy (if that is what you can really call them). Also with the fact that some of them tried to separate us, it being one of their unwritten laws that two alcoholics should not form a relationship.

Thank God we didn't follow their advice. We decided that we would try and overcome our problems together, not with a view to embracing life-long sobriety, but rather with a view to our both being free to be able to drink normally again.

I stress the 'again', because neither of us had always been alcoholic drinkers. In fact to start off with, both of us had been quite abstemious. I never drank at all as a teenager, and Murdoch used to tell me that when he was an undergraduate at university, he used to go for his lunch most days to a pub called *The Northampton Arms*, where his standing order was a round of cheese sandwiches and a small bottle of Mackeson stout. And, apart from the night before he got his MA degree, when he went out celebrating with his father, that was his sole alcoholic intake during his years at University.

Once as an undergraduate he had been accosted by an inebriated tramp begging for money. Murdoch replied: "If I were you, my good man, I would make the earliest possible appointment with my physician!" The tramp must have misheard, because, turning away in disgust, he mumbled: "Sorry guv, I ain't got no magician!"

We felt sure that drink was not the problem – drink had *become* a problem. If we could identify what had originally caused us to start drinking alcoholically, and deal with that, i.e. the real, underlying problem, the root cause, then the superficial, the merely (albeit serious) behavioural problem (i.e. the alcoholic drinking) would disappear of its own accord.

But in even believing this to be a possibility, we were apparently flying in the face not only of *Alcoholics Anonymous*, but also of some contemporary medical and psychiatric orthodoxy. Nobody seemed to believe that it could be done. Or, if they did, they were not prepared to say so. We do not believe that we are the first or the only people to have thought along these lines, but not ever having heard or read of their existence made our task a very lonely one. And one that was even more difficult than it might otherwise have been, if we had had any help or encouragement along the way, or the light of example of someone who had trod the same path before us.

We had noticed several instances in life of how, until somebody actually achieves something for the first time, it is popularly believed to be impossible. But as soon as one person does it, then suddenly it seems as though everyone who wants to, can do it. Before Roger Bannister first ran a mile in under four minutes, most other people (apart from him) thought that it would never be done. Similarly, Edmund Hilary and the conquest of Everest. It is doing these things for the first time that is the singularly difficult task. As soon as they are achieved and there is an example for others to follow, then they become commonplace, and no more noteworthy than a walk in the park.

It was just after four o'clock, and dinner was not until six, so we decided that we would now venture out for the short walk that we had planned earlier. Holding on tightly to each other, we wandered slowly down Castle Hill and across Chesterton Road, and then, on a sudden impulse, turned through the main gate of Murdoch's old college, Magdalene.

Term had not yet started, although it would the following week, so there was no one around at all, except for a porter sitting in the lodge, reading the evening paper. We walked through the first court, past the silent deserted chapel on the left, and into the cloisters outside the Great Hall. Murdoch had told me about the minstrels' gallery, and how, even now, dinner was taken by candlelight. But we weren't to see it at its best that day, because there was some renovation and redecoration going on. The floor was covered with dustsheets, while scaffolding scaled the walls.

One lonely light shone from a room in the Pepys library – some scholar was busy working over the weekend – as we slipped briefly into the Fellows' Garden. The peace and calm were overpowering, and we had to sit down for a few minutes to drink it in, and heal our wounded spirits.

We still had most of the ten cigarettes Murdoch had bought that morning, and we smoked one between us now as we savoured the silence. People had been sitting in that very garden for hundreds of years, but few could have drawn more spiritual comfort from the surroundings and the atmosphere than we did that evening.

Soon it was time to be going, as the college would be closing its gates for the night. On our way out, the porter gave us a cheerful but respectful wave from the lodge, and shouted goodnight. It was lucky that it was beginning to get dark, so that he probably couldn't see us too clearly, but his casual, friendly gesture gave us a warm glow, and helped us to feel a bit more human again.

Normally it would have been only a ten-minute walk back to the hostel, but Castle Hill is quite steep, especially on the way up, and as well as my aching swollen legs, I also had to contend with my burst shoes, which kept slipping off. Eventually I became so frustrated, that

I just took them off altogether, and walked the rest of the way in my bare feet.

We eventually arrived back at the hostel a couple of minutes before six o'clock, and dinner was just about to be served. The smell of the bolognese reminded us how hungry we were, but as soon as we entered the dining room and saw how busy it was, the panic attacks returned. But there was no way that we were going to leave that room before we had well and truly eaten, panic attacks or not!

I found a table where I could sit with my face to the wall, while Murdoch went up to the counter to collect our meals. Unfortunately he also had to collect two sweets, two cups of coffee, two napkins and various assorted cutlery, all precariously balanced on two plastic trays, so he was in quite a state when he returned, but I was shaking too much to sympathise.

Spaghetti is not the easiest thing to eat at the best of times, but how we managed that evening with the panic, the shakes and the sweats all increasing in intensity by the minute, I shall never know. But our extreme hunger came to our aid – all that was important was to get the pile of pasta, and as much of the sauce into our mouths by hook or by crook. Any pretence of gentility or decorum was thrown to the winds. We would have used shovels if necessary. But no one seemed to notice. Perhaps, for their own reasons everyone there was just as hungry as we were. And anyway, I don't think gentility and decorum are the commonest of currencies in homeless hostels.

We rapidly emptied our plates, including our sweet, although I don't remember much about that. What I do recall is the beautiful feeling of being full and replete for the first time in weeks. Our feeling of panic when we came into the dining hall had died down a bit, and this was perhaps an effect of the food, as it must muffle the jangling nerves.

After we had finished eating, we sat on for a bit, refilling our coffee cups as often as we could, for after this we would have nothing more until morning. When the jug was finally empty, we made our way back to the room with somewhat lighter hearts, and satisfyingly heavier stomachs.

It was a long evening, just our two selves with nothing to do. My television was still back at our old accommodation with our other belongings (a problem that would have to be sorted out on Monday). We both hated the inanity of Saturday night programmes, and we wouldn't normally have been viewing, but on that particular evening it would have broken the silence, and distracted us from the gloominess of our own thoughts.

We were still having to ration our cigarettes, of course – by now we only had four or five left – but just after ten o'clock we decided to share one between us down in the hostel garden. At least it would get us outside the four walls of that room, which were beginning to close in on us. Don't get me wrong, the room was reasonably sized, bright and pleasant enough, but any room, however pleasant, can become oppressive if you are stuck in it long enough with nowhere else to go.

As we sat in the garden taking a welcome puff, Julia and the rest of the day shift were preparing to leave, and the night shift taking over. Ermez, our friend from the night before, came round on his tour of inspection and stopped for a while to chat. He asked if we would like a cup of coffee, and we jumped at the chance. Murdoch went back with Ermez to the hostel office in the main building, and came back with two hot and steaming mugs, and in addition (what bliss!) two cigarettes from Ermez. Frugal as ever, we smoked just one of them between us with our coffee, and added the other to our dwindling stock. It was cold out there in the garden, but as we still had the sweats, it was a luxury, especially as we knew that we could go back into the warm any time that we wanted.

When he had finished his round of inspection, Ermez came back to collect our empty mugs, wished us goodnight, and we went back upstairs. Normally, coming off a bender, we would now face the prospect of several (in my case, many) sleepless nights, staring at the ceiling, one's mind racing with a jumble of thoughts and terrifying visions, but that night we were granted a temporary reprieve. Sleep came almost instantly, although it was the sleep of sheer exhaustion, and neither restful nor relaxing.

I was wakened suddenly; how long we had been sleeping I had no idea, to the sound of Murdoch shivering violently. The central heating was still on, and the room was warm and rather stuffy, but he insisted he was freezing cold. He seemed disorientated, and not sure where he was. I realised he was having a hallucination, and thought that we were still out in the open, sleeping rough. I hoped that this was not the start of the DTs, as these can be fatal. Strange as it may seem, coming off alcohol, especially when it is done too suddenly or without medical help, can be just as dangerous, or even more so, than carrying on drinking.

By now Murdoch had got himself fully dressed, and had even put his jacket and shoes on. He sat, trying to hug himself warm, whilst I was longing to open the window to get some cool fresh air, as the sweat was lashing off me. At last the crisis passed, Murdoch was eventually warm enough for me to open the window, and then I soon cooled off. We lay down again to try to sleep, which we managed to do fitfully, but it was a great relief when the first light of morning began to appear.

The world outside our window looked calm, peaceful, refreshed, and comfortingly normal. We didn't have much idea what time it was – Murdoch had lost his watch during the previous fortnight, so we dressed again, and walked slowly and stiffly over to the main block of the hostel. It was later than we thought, nearly eight o'clock, and as breakfast on Sunday was served at half-past eight, there were already several people about. There was even one man in the dining room sitting up at the table with his eating irons at the ready, tapping impatiently on the table, all the while gazing vacantly into the middle distance, whistling a sad little ditty slightly out of key.

Someone told us that he was always there in the same seat at the same table, at least an hour before every meal. His name was Charles, and we called him Charles of the Ritz. He didn't have a drink problem like us, but he did have a food problem. As far as Charles was concerned (and he was *very* concerned about it), food just never came quickly enough.

It certainly didn't that morning. News came filtering through that the chef had telephoned in to say that his car wouldn't start, and that he would not be in for another hour. Murdoch and I were disappointed, for the hunger pangs were beginning to gnaw again. But poor Charles! He looked as if the bottom had fallen out of his world. He was thoroughly bemused and crestfallen, as if Fate had dealt him a bewilderingly cruel blow, from which he would never fully recover, and the knife and fork in his fists beat out a mournful lament on the table, like the single monotonous beat of a drum following a hearse.

When we were at last summoned for a belated breakfast, we were sitting at our table drinking a last cup of coffee, when Julia came up and told us that there was an *AA* meeting in the centre of town that evening which was supposed to be quite good, and that, if we wanted to go, we could get a lift there and back afterwards.

Neither of us really wanted to go, but Julia said: "You know that neither of you can ever so much as sniff another drink again, and you're going to need all the help and support that you can get." So, in spite of what we had been saying to each other the previous day, we felt that we really had no alternative, and we agreed that we would go.

Suddenly I remembered my burst shoes, so I went to the hostel office and asked if I could borrow a needle and thread. As long as I could get someone to thread the needle, it would be quite easy for me to mend them, as they were light fashion shoes.

As Murdoch and I sat on a wooden bench in the sun, sewing the shoes between us, the distant memory of another pair of silver shoes came back into my mind.

I remembered back to when I was a child of about ten or eleven. My family lived in a mainly farming community. My father was not a farmer, but as a general dealer, he came into regular contact with those who were. Naturally therefore my parents always went to the Annual Farmers' Ball, and the invitation to that year's event had just been delivered to the house. My mother had bought a beautiful long red taffeta evening dress – the only evening dresses I had ever seen until then had been on television, never in real life.

That afternoon I was going to the Lochwinnoch Summer Fete, and was very excited at the prospect. I had been saving up my pocket money for several weeks, and I had about three shillings in old money to spend. There were pony rides, bottle and wheel of fortune stalls and coconut shies - I had a go on everything, as well as filling myself with ice cream, cakes and home-made tablet.

Then I spotted a display of second-hand books, clothes and shoes in an open tent. I wandered in, and bought a couple of annuals. All my money was just about gone, when suddenly I came across a huge basket of shoes. Rummaging through them, I found the most entrancing pair of silver dancing shoes that I could ever imagine. They were magical, fit only for a film star or a princess. I immediately thought of my mother going to the ball, and was determined to buy them for her.

The label on them said sixpence, so I counted out my last pennies and halfpennies, and found that there was just enough left. I asked the lady in charge if she would kindly wrap them up, and, when she had, I grabbed my treasured find with glee, and raced helter skelter homewards. I was bursting with joy, and could hardly wait to see my mother's face when she saw her present.

She was in the house by herself that late Saturday afternoon as I rushed in through the back door and shouted, "Mum!" at the top of my voice. She came out of the kitchen to see what all the commotion was about, and I said, "I've bought you a present, and you'll never guess what it is!" She smiled, and asked me to show her.

But as she unwrapped the parcel and saw what was inside, her expression changed instantly to one of fury. "What's this?" she thundered, picking up the shoes with the tips of her fingers and thrusting them in my face. "Don't you ever bring someone else's second-hand shoes into this house again. You never wear anyone else's shoes, you should know that. Any illnesses they've had go straight to their feet, and you'll catch them. Put these outside in the dustbin now!"

Outwardly I smiled, and did what she said, but inwardly I was fuming. She had never even tried them on! Silently, I spat the words "I hate you!" bitterly through my smile.

Re-wrapping the shoes in their newspaper, I took them outside as she had said, but later that day I secretly removed them from the dustbin, and hid them in the garden shed, underneath some of my father's tools.

To this day I still retain this strange affinity with all things silver, long dangly silver earrings, my long black and silver coat, and these battered silver shoes that I was mending now....

After the shoes we turned our attention to the splits in the seams and pockets of my silver and black coat, and once these repairs were complete, we took the coat up to the bathroom, gave it a good wash. Between us, we towel dried and squeezed it as best we could, and took it back down to the garden to hang and dry in the sun. Now, I thought, I would look reasonably respectable at the *AA* meeting that evening.

And as it turned out, I did, especially wearing my tinted reading glasses, which had remarkably come through the last few weeks in my bag unscathed, and some judiciously applied makeup.

We were picked up by car at about ten to seven, dropped in Emmanuel Street about twenty past, and pointed in the direction of the church hall where the meeting was held. But when we arrived, the doors were locked and the building was in darkness. Then along the street hurried a shortish slightly stooped figure with his long coat flapping behind him in the evening breeze. His hair was on the long side, with tufts brushed back over his ears, and he looked like a university professor rushing off to the lecture hall.

He introduced himself to us as Frank, and he was originally from America. He unlocked the door, and ushered us into a kitchen. There was a huge kettle that he filled, and put on the lighted gas to boil. Murdoch and I set out the cups as he made the tea, and we told him a bit about our story. One good thing about *AA* is that you can tell anybody anything, and know that they are not going to be shocked or judgmental, as they will either have been in a situation just as bad themselves, and maybe worse, or at least know plenty of other people who have.

As we sipped our tea, our hands still a bit shaky, other people began to arrive. They seemed equally friendly as Frank introduced us one by one. Then, just on time, we trooped into the meeting room itself. It was quite the most attractive *AA* venue that either of us has ever come across. It wasn't the church hall itself, just a large room off it. The appearance was of a minister's study or library, and was lined wall to wall with old leather-bound books. But best of all, candles burned in the old leaded windows, which had stained glass inlays of family coats-of-arms. The room was pervaded with a sense of perfect peace and tranquillity, and everybody shook our hand and wished us well.

The meeting ended on a distinctly pleasant note. As we were on our way out, Frank mentioned to me that there was nearly a pint of milk left, and asked whether it would be of any use to us. Not only that, but as we were shaking hands at the gate, I felt a piece of paper being pressed into my palm. It turned out, when we looked at it later, to be a five-pound note, for the loan of which we were truly grateful!

We got a lift back to the hostel as arranged, but instead of going straight in, we went round to the late-night grocers in Histon Road to spend our newly acquired riches. We bought twenty cigarettes (naturally!), a small jar of coffee, and a packet of chocolate biscuits (when I was drinking, or coming off a bender were the only times that I stopped worrying about my weight – I was too upset). Although we did our best to ration the cigarettes out, the whole lot, except five, had gone by morning.

We went back to that Sunday night *AA* meeting the following week, and took the opportunity to give Frank back his fiver. He didn't want to take it at first, but Murdoch pointed out that if we gave it back, Frank would be able to help somebody else whenever the opportunity arose, without himself being any more out of pocket.

We also went to several more *AA* meetings elsewhere in Cambridge, but however well-intentioned the people there were, and however grateful we might have been for their support and their company, we knew that, for reasons that I will explain more fully in due course, that we couldn't accept the basic ideas of the movement. So rather than cause any upset, we just stopped going.

That first weekend in the hostel, though completely uneventful, had at least given us the opportunity to get our thoughts together, and we had even begun to focus our minds once again on our own recovery. By Monday, the shakes and fears were not so bad, which was just as well, since we had all the practical tasks and administrative procedures to go through in order to try and repair some of the wreckage of the previous fortnight, and rejoin, if not the mainstream, at least a quiet backwater of the human race.

After breakfast, Julia brought us the good news that there was sufficient room for us to stay in the hostel for just as long as was necessary for us to get ourselves on our feet again, and come to some decisions about where we were going from there.

It might seem strange to you to read that a couple, who were both used to living in their own comfortable houses, should feel a sense of profound relief on being told that they were to be allowed to stay on in a homeless hostel. I can only tell you that it was exactly so. Our alcoholic drinking over twenty years in general, and this last nightmare bender in particular, had brought us down so low, that even this one small single step back towards normality seemed an unbelievable miracle.

There were innumerable forms to fill in. Julia took us into the office, and introduced us to Brian, who was to be our key worker during our stay. He was a tall, sturdy, amiable and easy-going man, with whom we both seemed to get on right from the start. He completed all the paperwork for us, as we were scarcely capable of even signing our own names. Just sitting there in that small confined office answering the questions that Brian put to us was a strain, the sweats and the shakes beginning to return, such are the after-effects coming off drink.

He explained that we could either pay for our food in the hostel out of our benefit giro, over and above what we would have to pay towards the cost of our rooms, or choose to go self-catering, and cook for ourselves in a communal kitchen/sitting-room. As I had a microwave, which was still back at our previous accommodation, we decided to take the self-catering option, which would also have the advantage of leaving us more money in our pockets.

At last it was all over, and we were officially residents of 222 Victoria Road, Cambridge.

We might have made a joke here, about there being a sign over the main door reading 'Abandon Hope All Ye Who Enter Here', but we would be the first to acknowledge that in fact the exact opposite was true. Bleak as our existence was to be in many ways over the next twelve months, nevertheless No. 222 was to be our way back to hope, our stepping-stone back to normality, and a vital staging post on our road to radical recovery. All the staff, and Brian in particular, gave us help and encouragement, sometimes above and beyond the call of duty, without which who knows whether or not this book would have come to be written?

Next Brian phoned a man with a van who he knew wouldn't charge us too much, to collect our luggage from the station, and we had that embarrassing encounter with the stationmaster that I've already described. And then back to our former lodgings to collect the rest of our belongings. Brian had also got us a lock-up from the council that we could use to store my furniture. Another five pounds a week to pay out, but we were quite delighted, as there was nothing else we could have done with it.

By the time we got back we were even more exhausted, but what bliss to have a clean change of clothes of our own to put on! We made ourselves a quick lunch in my room, which was about the size of a small prison cell – if you stretched your arms out sideways, you could touch both side walls at the same time. But we soon realised that we would have to keep the microwave in it, as well as store our food there, as we had been warned that anything we left in the communal kitchen would magically disappear. After eating, we decided to take a brief but well-deserved rest.

We were beginning to worry about how much we were going to be paying out for our new refuge, but now that fate had decided to take a hand in our affairs and work in our favour, she wasn't going to leave things alone for long. As if by chance, someone had given us a copy of the early edition of that day's *Cambridge Evening News*. He had bought it for the racing page, and, having chosen his bets for the afternoon, was finished with it. Murdoch was leafing idly through it, when suddenly he nudged me. "Hey, look at this!"

He was pointing at an advertisement in the recruitment pages, and I started to read it. It was offering a job selling newspapers on the street, so my immediate reaction was not very keen.

"But everyone will see us!" I objected, but then I thought, well, that didn't really bother us too much during the previous two weeks, while we were roaming around the town, openly drinking. Had we thought we were invisible then? At least now we would be seen trying to do an honest day's work. Admittedly not exactly the sort of work that Murdoch's degree had fitted him for, but at least it would be a start, and we would be able to put some money away, hopefully, in preparation for whatever we eventually decided to do next.

The advertisement gave a telephone number, and the name of Barry Rowe to ring if you were interested. By this time we were. In fact we were getting quite excited, and in our mind's eye, we could already see Murdoch doing the job, standing on a street corner shouting: "Read all about it! *Cambridge Evening News*!" at the top of his voice.

But we came back down to earth. Murdoch took a couple of ten pence pieces and went downstairs to the main entrance where there was a payphone. He came back, having made the call, with a smile on his face. He had arranged an interview with Barry Rowe the following afternoon. The 24-hour delay was in our favour, as by the next day we would both be feeling that much better.

While Murdoch went into our shared kitchen to make us a celebratory cup of coffee, I took a look at the newspaper myself, and came across something almost equally as interesting. There was a long article in the centre spread under the headline "Shame on you, Cambridge!" and lo and behold, it was all about the young 'tramp' we met in Market Square that fateful Friday night, and whose blanket we had nearly stolen.

The article was not by a journalist, but by a lady member of the public who had befriended James the previous week, and had a long talk with him. She was berating the medical and social services of Cambridge for cruelly ignoring his silently uncomplaining plight, when he was so obviously seriously ill.

From our own experience we could agree with what she had written. The local hospitals refused to have anything to do with alcoholics, unless and until, as a doctor had told us, they became really critically ill. But how critical is critical? James had told us that he had chronic liver disease, and was now suffering alcoholic paralysis, which was keeping him virtually a prisoner on a public bench with winter approaching, and practically everyone ignoring him.

It was still not much more than four o'clock in the afternoon, so we decided to take a walk down to Market Square before dinner, to see James and find out whether there was anything we could do for him.

Perhaps, if he was well enough, a place might be found for him at the hostel. But we were too late.

There was no one at all on the bench by the side of the Guildhall where we had seen him before. It was completely empty. Empty, that is, except for a scrap of paper on which two oranges had been placed. Visible on the scrap of paper was a child's handwriting. It simply said, 'From a friend.'

We never did find out what became of James. We hope that the article in the *Cambridge Evening News* had shamed the hospital authorities into sending out an ambulance to fetch him in for treatment. But we wouldn't be too sure. Without help, anything could have happened to him. Alcoholics are very vulnerable – prey to accident as well as illness. They can cure themselves, as we shall show, but often some sort of intervention is required to enable them to get off the treadmill, and into a position where they can begin to work out their own salvation. Such an intervention had occurred for us. We hope it did for James.

Next day Murdoch was to go for his meeting with Barry Rowe at the *Cambridge Evening News*. Neither of us felt anywhere near a hundred per cent yet – we always reckoned that it took us at least the same length of time to get over the after-effects of a bender as we had spent drinking whilst we were on it. But if you need or want something badly enough, it's amazing how you can psych yourself up to putting on a convincing enough performance, as long as it doesn't have to last too long!

After lunch at the hostel I decided that I would take a walk down with Murdoch, and wait outside for him while he was having his interview. That way I would get to know the outcome almost as soon as he did.

At that time the newspaper was still housed in its old building a mile or so from the city centre along Newmarket Road, but rather than go into town, we opted for the back way – down to the bottom of Victoria Road, across the double roundabout, over the River Cam and through Midsummer Common. It was a mild afternoon, and we found a seat where we could enjoy a cigarette before Murdoch went round the corner into Newmarket Road in order to keep his appointment on time. I had brought a book with me to help pass the time, and settled down to wait for his return.

Not surprisingly, he wasn't long. After all, how many questions are there you can ask someone who only wants a job selling newspapers? Apart from, why the hell do they want to do it in the first place?

"Please sir, because I'm desperate."

"Oh well, right ho then!"

Murdoch was smiling, so I knew that the news was good. It was. He and Barry had got on well, he had been offered the job, and was starting the very next day. One small step in the career of a news vendor, a giant stride forward on our road to recovery!

We were talking excitedly (you'd have thought we'd landed the chairmanship of ICI, at least) and found ourselves back along Newmarket Road and into Bridge Street before we knew it. Murdoch said he would show me his new 'pitch', and led me round the back of Eaden Lilley's department store, past the Arts Cinema and into Market Square. Fifty yards up to the right, there it was, at the end of Rose Crescent, an unmanned, deserted newspaper stand, which as from the next day would be ours. What was strange was that, at the *Cambridge Evening News*, this particular "pitch" was known as "McDonald's Corner", not, admittedly, in honour of us, but probably more likely because there was a McDonald's restaurant in Rose Crescent. Nevertheless, it was a strange coincidence.

So from then on, although it was officially Murdoch's job, we were, in fact virtually a working couple. Straight after breakfast he would count up his takings from the previous day and write up his return sheet. Then he had a two-mile hike to the newspaper offices to hand them in to Barry (on the first morning it was just to receive last minute instructions). Thence to King Street, opposite *The Bun* public house, where (for some reason unknown) all the news vendors collected their first delivery of the early edition. Then, humping a quire or two of heavy newspapers, he would set off for his pitch in Market Square, and set up his stall for the day.

Sometime between eleven o'clock and noon I would set off from the hostel to join him for a while and give him some company (it could be a long, cold and lonely job). Also to take him some sandwiches and a flask of hot tea. That first morning I was taking him his lunch, and as I turned out of Trinity Street into Rose Crescent I could hear Murdoch shouting at the top of his voice, but in his best BBC accent, "Early Edition! *Cambridge Evening News!*" Just for a moment I felt very sad, and thought of why we had come to Cambridge in the first place, for Murdoch to study for his PhD. We would only be one year married the following Christmas Eve, and this was not the way it was supposed to be. But it was the way things had turned out, so now we had to make the best of it, and work to get back on our feet.

At the time as I caught sight of Murdoch, he looked up, saw me, smiled and waved. He looked cheerful, but you could tell he was not well. He was too thin, had lost nearly a stone in weight, and his face was ashen grey. But we were glad to see each other, and be back together again.

The other reason I made my twice-daily pilgrimages (I used to go back to the hostel in between times for my own lunch) was the very basic one of manning the news stand to relieve Murdoch and allow him to slip away to the public toilet in Lion's Yard. I don't know how the other vendors managed, but we amused ourselves imagining how one of them did.

Joyce was an old lady in her seventies who had been selling newspapers on the same 'pitch' on the corner of Hobson's Passage near to Waterstone's bookshop every day, come wind, rain, hail or snow for more than forty years. We had passed her many times since we had first arrived in Cambridge, but not once had I ever seen her move from her seat. Once I had happened to remark to Murdoch, "I wonder if that's a chair she's sitting on, or is it really a commode?" At that very moment, Joyce uncrossed her legs, the great buttocks shifted, and her grim scowl intensified. We were left wondering...

One of the first times that I was standing on our 'pitch' alone, having let Murdoch away for a quick toilet break, Barry Rowe marched up and introduced himself. He was about our own age, or perhaps a few years younger, and had joined the newspaper after leaving the Army as a staff sergeant.

Apart from the fact that he no longer wore a khaki uniform, he still had a military air about him as he marched around Cambridge, marshalling his troop of newsvendors, and exhorting them to ever greater efforts in his ceaseless battle to increase sales. He always carried a clipboard, and from it he could tell you in a moment how many newspapers had been sold on each 'pitch' on any particular day during the previous five years. His statistics were already telling him that Murdoch's sales were way above average.

Another time that I was at the stand with Murdoch, two of our former drinking companions from Christ's Pieces came up to speak to us. They said they hardly recognised us, seemed very impressed with our new job, and thought that we had really gone up in the world. "You'll be voting bloody Tory next!" one said.

So that was the pattern of our days set for the time being. We were working all day, but after dinner at the hostel in the evening we were free. We have never been great television watchers, so we spent the greater part of those lengthening winter evenings, closeted in our room, which I had managed to make reasonably cosy, engaged in long, and often earnest discussions, trying desperately to solve our common problem, 'alcoholism'.

We were still convinced, in spite of all our setbacks along the way, that life-long sobriety could not be the final solution. It could only be a means to an end, a period of respite during which one could calmly and clearheadedly address and analyse the real underlying problems.

Having isolated and recognised what those problems were, and solved them, one could then be free to drink normally again, if one so wished.

I knew that I had been unhappy with myself long before alcohol had become a problem. We were totally convinced that both the real underlying problems and the answers lie in one's childhood. (Where else could they be? One thing we all have in common is that we have all been children, and that our past creates our future.) So that was where we should start to put it all together. And that is what we did.

Right from when we first met, Murdoch was the first person who ever really listened to me, and what I had to say, and that meant a lot to me. One thing I did know was that he was intelligent. More importantly, he was the first person to tell me that I was intelligent as well – as he explained, it was a largely a matter of having an enquiring mind. Don't get me wrong – I am only of average intelligence, but that was enough.

No matter how intelligent you are, it won't stop you becoming an 'alcoholic', but an enquiring mind will help you to understand yourself, and hopefully to work out the solution to your problems.

I had always confused intelligence with being clever. But they are not the same at all – a lot of clever people can understand what you're saying, but some are too lazy to go back and put it all together, even when you give them the answers. There are others who don't listen – it just goes straight over their head. They're taking the easy way out; it's so much easier to stay the same. And then there are those who have a false arrogance, and who resent being told, especially when they're having a fairly good day, and they think they know all the answers. They're afraid to show their vulnerable side. And finally, there will always be some unfortunate people who wouldn't be able to do it for other reasons.

But more importantly, prevention is better than any cure. These self-harming behaviour problems shouldn't be happening in the first place.

Murdoch listening to me had begun to give me back a bit of my self-confidence, me who had for so long now been riddled with self-doubt. I started to believe in myself, and to trust my intuition, which I understand as meaning 'being in touch and in tune with yourself'. Because I had never been at peace with myself before, I had always been afraid to challenge other people's opinions, and had never had the confidence or self-assertion to believe in what I thought was important and listen to and trust my own feelings.

So I related my life story to Murdoch, albeit in bits and pieces. Previously I had not been able to tie my whole life up and bring it all together, but with Murdoch's help, over time I was able to do just that…

Chapter Three
Lilian's Story

Happy families are all alike; every unhappy
family is unhappy in its own way.

Leo Tolstoi: ***Anna Karenina***

AS a child, I do not ever remember being happy at home. In the house,
it was as if a dark dreary cloud came over my life, there was no joy at
all. The only fun and happiness I recall was that which I created for
myself whenever I was out of doors.

Then I was a real scamp, getting up to every kind of innocent mischief that I could possibly devise. At times when I was compelled to
remain indoors, either by parental command, inclement weather, or
dark winter evenings, I developed my own pursuits which served the
double purpose of passing the time of my confinement as pleasantly as
possible, and of avoiding the notice, and any adverse or critical comment, from my mother or father.

I taught myself embroidery, and would sit silently sewing for hours
on end, while my thoughts could wander freely wherever they wished.
As far as my parents were concerned, I was in the house, where they
could keep an eye on me, was behaving, and even, seemingly, doing
something reasonably useful. Inwardly, they breathed a sigh of relief,
tiptoed around me, and left me in heavenly peace. There are more ways
of achieving escape and oblivion than just by drinking alcoholically.

I was the middle of three children; Gordon was two years older, and Elsie two years younger. I do not remember sharing any fun with either of them, and it seems as if we must have inhabited separate, but parallel universes, or at least as if we were not really siblings at all (my mother always said that she thought I must be a throw-back to a previous generation of the family), but just three unrelated children who happened to be living in the same house. But although our blood relationship was never in question, as children there was never any real bond between us.

All I remember is that, whenever Elsie fell out with me, Gordon would take her side, and when I fell out with my brother, she would take his side. There was never any enmity between us; I was just the odd one out. "That one's the rebel in this family," was another thing my mother used to say about me. Whereas Elsie willingly chose to become a Sunday school teacher, and Gordon was renowned for his quiet obedience, my mother had to force me to go to Church.

From the age of about eight until I was twelve, I had to go to Sunday School in the morning, and then in the afternoon it was the Plymouth Brethren meetings. When I was thirteen I was told to join the Church, and around fourteen or fifteen the Youth Fellowship on Sunday evenings was added to my list of obligations. Even when I was about sixteen, I wasn't allowed to go to a dance unless it was organised by the Church. However, one thing I noticed was that neither of my mother nor my father ever attended any Sunday services, but I wouldn't have been allowed to say anything about this. I knew what the answer would have been: "Don't do as I do, do what I tell you!" If I ever tried to disagree, I was firmly told that my opinions didn't matter.

So my Sundays were fully accounted for, or so my parents thought! There was a small cinema in the village, The Palace, also known as Johnny's, after Johnny Manders, the owner. It started to open on a Sunday evening, and that was where I wanted to be, with my friends. We didn't have to ask our parents for money, as at that time you could get in to the cheap seats in the stalls for a couple of empty lemonade bottles. Johnny would then get the deposit money back on them.

So some weeks I would chance it, and give the Youth Fellowship a miss. They were too stuffy for me there. As soon as I got into the cinema, I would go to the ladies cloakroom, perform a magician's trick, and come out a painted doll. After the evening performance was over, all the make-up had to be scrubbed off under the lamplight outside, before I could dare show my face back home.

There was also a café with a jukebox in the village, where all my friends would meet, but this was supposed to be strictly out of bounds for me in the evening, as my father thought that it was just the local riffraff who went there. Needless to say, I would sneak in there whenever I could, sandwiching myself in the midst of my friends so that I wouldn't be visible from the street outside.

Unfortunately, one summer evening I was just getting up to play the jukebox with a glass of orange juice in my hand, when my father came into the café to buy some ice cream. I was wearing a huge pair of flashy earrings and loads of make-up, of course, but it was my father's face that was the real picture. He was livid, and gave me a thorough dressing-down in front of my friends, and then ordered me home immediately.

Once my parents were going away for a few days, and my brother was left in charge. As soon as the car disappeared down the drive, out came my cigarettes, and then I dashed to the telephone to invite all my friends round for a party. I got my mother's good crystal glasses out and filled them with lemonade, pretending it was champagne. Straight to the kitchen after that. Then out came the frying pan, and as we all tucked into a gigantic fry-up, Gordon sat petrified on the settee in his neatly pressed trousers, polished brown brogues and Fair Isle jumper. "Do you really *like* living dangerously?" he eventually ventured to ask. The answer was yes – I just wanted fun, and to hell with the consequences.

I thought that we were a very respectable family, living in a very respectable village. Lochwinnoch, along with the neighbouring Renfrewshire villages of Kilmacolm and Bridge of Weir were apparently considered (and probably still are) rather desirable places to live. Much more so than across the valley in Kilbirnie and Glengarnock, the site of the local steelworks.

As far as I was concerned, I just loved the nearby countryside, where I could help out on the farms, where I was allowed to go, only because my father knew most of the farmers well. Especially I loved the smell of barns and haylofts, and of hen houses and chicken coops when I went to collect the eggs. These smells were more precious to me than the most expensive perfume, and I treasure the memory of them still.

I can still see quite clearly in my mind's eye today one particular hayloft with a window just beneath the eaves. A ray of sunlight angled in, and caught the specks of grain-dust dancing in its beam. I was warmed by the comfortable homeliness of the farmhouse kitchens with their home-made butter and cheese, the welcome that you got there, and the farmers' easy friendly ways. Most of them didn't mind if there was a bit of dung sticking to my Wellington boots – it wasn't that important.

At home it was the opposite. Outwardly everything was fine. It had to be, because appearances were all-important. My father wore his respectability like a second skin, he never took it off. His mask of correctness was never allowed to slip. If anything it was even more firmly fixed in place at home than in the world outside. He always gave me the impression that he thought that our family was a cut above everybody else (though for the life of me I couldn't imagine why – we were just an ordinary family), and his regular exhortation to me was, "Always remember who you are!"

My father worked long hours, seven days a week, building up his business. I never once heard him complain – if he had a bad day, well, he had a bad day, that was all. There was always the next one. Neither did he ever ask for anything for himself, although every Saturday night at the end of his working week, he did treat himself to a double nougat ice cream wafer. Then it was back to work on the Sunday. He came from a family of market gardeners, whose rule had always been, "If you don't work, you don't eat." That was the rule in our house, too – we were all expected to pull our weight.

"Duty calls!" was another of his favourite phrases. Duty was everything. Even when he came back home from work in the evening, he would disappear after dinner and write up his accounts for a couple of hours.

Materially speaking, he was an excellent parent, and he was a good provider. We always had plenty of good food, warmth and clothes. We always had a car (not all that common in those days), were taken on holidays every year, and were amongst the first in the village to have a telephone. But we were emotionally and intellectually starved. No explanations for anything were ever offered, none of my own individual and personal opinions were ever tolerated, and questions were certainly not allowed.

This was doubly unfortunate for me since, almost as if I was a budding journalist in the making, questions were my forte, my stock-in-trade. Who? What? Where? When? How? But the greatest of these was *WHY*? I must have been persistent, because it came to the point where my mother, before taking me out anywhere, would give my sleeve a tug and warn me, "I'm telling you this before we go. If we meet any one to speak to, don't you dare start asking any questions. Just keep quiet, and do as you're told. And most of all, don't keep asking *why!*" And this I took very seriously, especially coupled with my grandmother's frequent warnings to me that 'curiosity killed the cat!'

Sometimes if there was something I wanted to know, I would try to get my mother's attention by pulling at her skirt. But she always seemed to be too busy, and just gave me a row for crumpling her clothes.

When I was about twelve years old, at the local village school, we had knitting lessons once or twice a week. At this particular time we were being taught how to knit scarves. Unfortunately, I had not understood the teacher Mrs Love's original instructions, and was too frightened to ask her to tell me again. So as the rest of the class started knitting away busily (they soon had about twelve inches done), I hid myself away in the middle of the classroom clicking away my needles industriously, but managing only to produce a hopeless muddle with a hole in it.

I succeeded in concealing my failure for some considerable time, but eventually on one of her tours of inspection, the teacher asked me to hold up my work. She was obviously shocked by my paltry efforts. "Why didn't you ask if you didn't understand?" she demanded. "Please miss, I'm not allowed to ask questions," I replied. She just looked at me. "Stupid girl," she said.

It only takes a second to hurt a sensitive child. In a blink it's gone, put to the back of your mind, but never truly forgotten.

But in a material way, my mother, like my father, was an excellent parent. She hand-knitted all our vests herself, as well as our socks, scarves, gloves and pixie hats, and all our bought clothes were of the best quality. Her home baking was a regular treat, and the house was always kept clean, even to the point of obsession. She would make us stand in one spot while she vacuumed around us, then we would have to move so that she could vacuum where we'd stood before. Even a few occasional stray crumbs were never allowed to lie, they were swept up immediately.

There was always an abundance of fresh fruit in the house, laid out in cut-glass bowls, so we never went hungry, even between meals, although we would always need to ask permission before we took anything to eat. At night, we would be lined up to be given our dose of cod liver oil, followed by a sweet to take away the revolting taste, and then milk and biscuits for our supper. Lastly, our faces scrubbed until they shone, our hair fragrant and neatly combed, our countenances divine lit up by three angelic smiles, my mother presented us to our father to say goodnight.

Unfortunately, I don't suppose he ever even noticed. He would have taken all this for granted, because that was how he thought all perfect families were. And he certainly would have thought that we were a perfect family. You would have offended his sense of propriety if you had dared to suggest that we were not.

He would come home from work some days, and I would be quietly reading, sitting in his chair – the one nearest the fire, and the best chair in the house. Sometimes he let me stay where I was – on other occasions the 'how dare you!' look on his face was enough to make me jump up and vacate my seat.

I was also expected to be clever at school, but he never involved himself with any of my homework. I remember once he was not very pleased that I had received a bad report card. Not long after, he came in with a complete twelve-volume set of encyclopaedias, and proudly cleared a shelf for them in the living room. "Now, get on and read those," he said proudly – and then he was gone. That was him sorting out the problem, but even more importantly, the encyclopaedias were on display for everyone to see, proving that he was a conscientious parent.

So my mother's days seemed an endless round of washing, cooking, ironing, cleaning, baking, knitting and sewing. She would never have taken the time for an individual personal life of her own. Her whole world revolved inexorably around that of my father, and everything she did was expressly designed in subservience to his wish, command or convenience.

But, as I've said, he probably never even noticed. More to the point he probably didn't want to notice. And because he didn't want to notice, he preferred nothing to be brought to his attention. Nothing was allowed to be wrong with us. I don't mean illnesses – obviously the normal childhood ailments, measles, mumps and chickenpox, they were only to be expected, and duly treated by our family doctor. But emotional matters, unhappiness, discontent even, depression certainly, these were not permitted to exist, or if they did dare to raise their ugly head, then they were rightly and properly ignored. All was for the best in this, the best of all possible homes. Even after I left home and was married, there remained an invisible sign on their front door, which read: "If you have any problems – don't bring them in here!"

Much later in life, shortly before he died in fact, I caught him out exercising his emotional myopia. Whenever he came round to my house, one of the first things he would say was, "Well, how are we today?" Just once, instead of the usual "Fine. Just fine," it suddenly popped into my head to say, "Not so good. In fact, I died this morning." But he was still as impervious as ever. Back came his habitual, inevitable response: "Good, good. That's what I like to hear." As far as emotional matters were concerned, not only was he short-sighted. He was obviously hard-of-hearing as well.

My childhood home was not so much a home as a mechanical house, and we were a family acting out our regimented lives within it. Mealtimes were arranged to suit my father's work schedule, and were not the happy times of relaxed enjoyment I imagined other families had. Every day we had to sit up straight, elbows off the table, don't slouch, don't speak with your mouth full, go easy on the condiments, and hold your utensils in the correct manner – ("it's a knife, not a pencil, don't saw your meat, cut it!") then stand up in turn to ask politely for permission before we left the table.

We were never allowed to keep pets as some other children did, because dogs had dirty paws, and cats scratched the furniture and carpets. I never felt free to invite any of my friends around for tea. It wasn't that it was expressly forbidden – if the truth were known, I would have felt embarrassed and uncomfortable for them to experience what my home and family were like, and I much preferred to go to their houses to play.

There was one friend in particular, Margaret McConnell, in whose house I loved to spend a lot of time. There were four children in that family, but there was always room for one more when I was visiting. I felt welcome and wanted in her home, as I did not in my own. We could play with all our toys spread out upon the carpet (bagatelle was our favourite, as I remember), without fear of recrimination, and we could make cups of tea, or help ourselves to orange juice and biscuits without being obliged to submit a formal request beforehand. Nobody was bothering over much about being perfectly correct at all times, and I just felt at home, and comfortably at ease.

Margaret's mother would as often as not be in the same room with us, sitting at her treadle sewing machine, making curtains or whatever. From time to time threads would drop upon the carpet. I would watch this, fascinated, and never failed to be surprised that she was not constantly jumping to her feet to pick them up, as my own mother would have done. She just let them lie, and carried on calmly and unruffled with whatever she was doing.

Later in the afternoon I would do all I could to help her with the preparations for the family's evening meal, hoping against hope that I would be invited to stay, and, of course, I usually was. As soon as Margaret's father Jock walked through the front door, the first thing he did was to fling wide his arms, and all of us children would rush to welcome him, and share in his embrace. Myself included, and this made me feel more at home with this family than I was with my own.

During the meal everyone would be chattering cheerfully to and fro across the table – I was unaccustomed to so much jovial repartee. After we had all finished eating, we would all go back through to the sitting room, where Margaret's father would sit in his favourite easy chair in front of the coal fire and light up his pipe. Then, with Margaret sitting on his knee, her sister curled over a chair arm, and me lying on the carpet at his feet, he would ask us all in turn how we were, and how our day had been. He asked as if he really cared, because of course he really did.

Then came the part that we all liked the best. He told us all about his day, and then went on to tell us stories, whilst we all sat or lay intently listening, watching the smoke from his pipe waft lazily up towards the ceiling. I felt important in that house, just as all that family did amongst themselves.

Unlike Margaret's father, my own was autocratic rather than democratic as far as his family was concerned. He ruled us rather than raised us. But make no mistake, I idolised him, although his daughter's love seemed to pass unnoticed by him, like everything else in the emotional sphere.

As a family we did not eat out all that often, and when we did it was a special occasion. There was one such celebration when we all went out to high tea. I remember the waitress's prim black dress and starched white headband, and when it came to my turn, I felt very grand as she asked me what it was that I would like to eat. I didn't need to think, and my answer was short and to the point.

"I want what my daddy's having, please," I said, smiling a little proudly. The waitress smiled too, while she wrote in her note-pad. As soon as her back was turned, I scampered round to the head of the table where my father was sitting, and tugged impatiently at his sleeve.

"Daddy, daddy! I'm having the same as you! I've told the lady so!" The disdain on his face had to be seen to be believed. He didn't even look in my direction, his hand just flapped at me dismissively. He tut-tutted in annoyance. "Go and sit down!" he said.

It was as if I had been slapped hard in the face. My eyes stung, my cheeks blushing, and, smiling my habitual response, I returned defeated and humiliated to my seat. I had been made to feel as though I had done something dreadfully wrong (again!) but could not seem to be able to begin to work out why. And my older brother sniggering at me, and making me feel stupid made things worse.

I used to spend as much time as I could as a child out and away from Bleak House, playing either with my friends, or, when they had all gone back home to their families, just by myself on my own.

I realise now that perhaps my father too, working his long hours, had found his own means of escape from the domestic environment, which he probably also, in his particular, similar, but different adult way, found too confining and restricting. He had made all the rules, but having done so, he was bound by them as much as anyone, perhaps even more so. Demanding perfection from his family, he had to appear even better than perfect to us. He was imprisoned in a cell of his own construction, but at least he had a pass-key, and was granted a regular taste of temporary freedom, for the duration of his working day.

During my all too short hours of freedom roaming Lochwinnoch, the leader of a faithful gang, hell-bent in search of ever more mischief to get up to, one of my favourite escapades was called 'chap door – run fast'. For this, all that was required was two front doors exactly opposite each other, a length of strong rope or heavy string, and most important, an ability to sprint.

None of these presented us with any problem whatsoever. There were plenty of narrow entrances to flats off the village high street, which gave us ample territory to choose from, and I could always find rope and string lying around in my father's yard. As for the ability to sprint, either you had it or you didn't, and fortunately my gang and I had it. We had to have.

The trick was to find two front doors not only facing each other, but ones where there were lights on, indicating there was someone at home. We would tiptoe up to the chosen front doors, tie one end of the rope tightly to each doorknocker, leaving exactly the right amount of slack in order to achieve the maximum mayhem. When everything was in place and arranged to my complete satisfaction, I gave the signal for the real operation to begin. We would chap (knock) urgently and thunderously upon each door simultaneously, as if to announce the outbreak of World War Three, and then run fast, making our most rapid possible escape to a suitable vantage point, from which we could view at our leisure the pleasurable results of our misdeeds.

As the first door was opened inwards, it took up the slack in the rope, so that when the second door was opened shortly afterwards, the first door slammed shut, the handle ripped violently from the occupant's hand, much to his or her bafflement and bewilderment. That was when the tug-of-war really began, with the first door being re-opened and the second one slamming shut. Then to and fro it went, amidst a mounting tide of blasphemy and other foul and obscene language, which, if nothing else, contributed substantially to our growing fund of knowledge acquired in the course of our extra-curricular education.

It was surprising how long this spectacle sometimes continued, as one door opened, another one slammed in somebody's face. Amazing how long it sometimes took people, like mice caught in a maze, to figure out the cause of their predicament. Eventually they always did, but by that time my friends and I had melted silently away into the background of the surrounding hills.

Not all my sports were so confederate – sometimes I played a solitary game. Once on a winter's day, the loch was completely frozen over, and deep snow covered the countryside for as far as the eye could see. It was in the Christmas school holidays, and it seemed as though all the children in Lochwinnoch had turned out, as we always did each year whenever a freeze like this occurred, coercing as many adults as possible to accompany us, to supervise and provide us with sustenance and provisions. There was always plenty of hot soup, tea, sandwiches and biscuits, to keep us warm and renew our energy. Suitably fortified, we would throw ourselves into the fray. Some brought sledges, others skated on the ice. We all had to be careful of the local swans, which tended to be a bit bad-tempered and pecky at their territory being invaded. They slipped and slided just as much as we did on the icy surface, as everywhere the sound of shouts and laughter echoed round the valley all day long.

But long after everyone else had departed and returned to their homes, when the sun like a giant blood orange was slowly bobbing down onto the horizon, I was still out in the hills on my own, furiously scrabbling together a giant snowman. By the time he was finished, he was at least a foot taller than I was myself, but my task was not yet completed.

From a sack I took out an old cap and muffler from our jumble box at home, and put them on my new creation. Also in my sack was a bundle of old oily rags, and these together with a pile of brushwood gathered from around about, I piled up on all sides of my snowman, as he gazed past me, apparently totally unconcerned. I took a twig of wood and put it in his mouth – the condemned man was granted a last cigarette.

The brushwood was by now surrounding him up to his shoulders, and I was ready for the climax of my ceremony. I took out a box of matches I had stolen from the kitchen earlier, and started the conflagration of the funeral pyre. Thanks to the oily rags it started quickly, and was soon burning beautifully. It was time for me to make my escape.

At the same time as I was making my way homewards, I learned afterwards that my father happened to be standing by the kitchen window, idly looking out towards the hills. He pointed out to my mother the unaccustomed glow on the horizon, and asked her what she thought it might be. I do not think he ever found out what (or who) was the cause. And, if he had, perhaps he would have preferred not to....

So both my father and I, in our different ways, both found a means of escape, temporary as it was, from Colditz Castle. We were both rebels for the same cause. I just wished that we could have joined forces, and fought side by side in the same battle. Unfortunately, he couldn't (wouldn't) see that there was a battle at all. He would have found the whole idea fanciful and ridiculous, and dismissed it with contempt. So I was condemned to fight on alone, not as a soldier in open warfare, but as a secret agent, achieving my clandestine aims by stealth and subterfuge.

My abiding ambition was to be allowed to accompany my father to his work, even if it was only for one day, and would constantly and repeatedly badger him to let me do so. My efforts were always in vain, however, being countered with various evasive tactics such as "One day, maybe," "We'll see," and "Don't be so stupid," or just simply "No."

One day, I could stand this no longer, and decided to make a sortie behind the battle lines, and right into enemy territory. At that time my father drove a lorry, delivering feed and other supplies to the local farms. Straight after breakfast, while he was getting himself ready for work, I went and hid myself in the driver's cab. I took an old copy of the *Glasgow Herald* from beneath the dashboard, opened it out, and held it up in front of me, thinking that this would prevent my father from seeing me, and realising that I was there. I was shortly to discover however that such cloaks of invisibility might work exceedingly well in fairy stories or myths, but unfortunately were not nearly so effective in real life.

It was ironic that the one and only time that I did not want my father to notice me was one of the very few times that he did.

My ejection from his cab was decisive and summary. Instead of being given the opportunity of sharing his adventures along the road, I was banished back to my everyday existence, wiling away another Saturday with second-best companions, and second-best escapades that would have to make do.

There were other big disappointments as well. Often when we had a school play or concert in the village hall, I would ask my mother and father to come and see me take part. All they would ever say was: "We'll see." After the performance ended, and the house lights went up, I would excitedly scan the audience from the stage, hoping against hope that at least one of them might be there. But they never were.

My mother used to say to me that school days were the happiest days of your life, and that worried me. I used to ask all my friends whether they were happy, because I did not know what happiness felt like.

When my parents had both died, I used to think of my father practically every day, whereas of my mother barely at all. When the memory of her does come back to me, it is just her expressionless face I see, no smile, and with nothing to say to each other. But my father I think of more often, although less frequently now that I have moved on. I tell him things I think or do, and share with him things I feel. Although he is dead, I can now allow him to be a companion in some of my adventures in life, a favour which I regret, when he was alive, he could never extend to me.

Although my father was the symbol of the oppression I felt as a child at home, and was the ultimate source of it, he also increased the insecurities of my mother, who was the agent through whom I actually felt my father's rule of law most strongly.

But my mother's insecurities can be traced back to her childhood.

Her father had been a habitual womaniser, who eventually deserted his family when my mother was still only about eight years old. Her own mother, Lily Ann, after whom I was named, died soon afterwards, apparently of a broken heart.

The two children, Ida (my mother) and her brother Jim were left helpless and alone, effectively orphaned. A crisis conference was called, which all the family solemnly attended, and before which Ida and Jim were made to stand, as if they were on trial. Which in a way they were, as their very future was being decided upon.

Each relative in turn gave unselfish-sounding reasons why it would not be in the best interests of either child to come and live with them. But behind the hypocritical pretence it was patently obvious, especially, probably, to the children themselves, that none of the family had the slightest wish or intention of being burdened with either of them.

Finally it occurred to one of her aunts that Jim, being considerably older than Ida, was old enough to be sent out to work, and far from being a cause of additional expense, could actually prove to be a source of extra income, so he quickly found a berth. Over Ida, however, there was much further wailing and gnashing of teeth, until at last her grandmother, bitterly complaining about the cost and the inconvenience, reluctantly agreed to take my mother. But, possibly regretting that she had not got in first with an offer for the more remunerative brother, added a grim and foreboding condition: "If she comes to me, she'll have to work hard to earn her keep!"

And work hard my mother certainly had to. She waited on her grand-mother hand and foot, although by this time slavery was supposed to have been abolished. Unfortunately, someone would appear to have neglected to inform my mother's self-appointed guardian.

So, constantly reminded of her dependent position, Ida was forced to continue performing every menial task that her grandmother could think of imposing upon her, right up until the day she left the house, against her grandmother's wishes, to marry my father.

As for Jim, he escaped and ran away, stowing away on board a ship bound for Montreal, entering Canada as an illegal immigrant. He wrote, once, to my mother, telling her what he had done, and promising faith-fully to come back to bring her over to Canada to join him, just as soon (to quote his own words) 'he had made it big.'

After that, nothing. She never heard from him again. Years later, she spent much time and trouble trying to trace her brother, and find out what had happened to him. At long last, shortly before she herself died, she received a letter from the Salvation Army.

Jim had died an alcoholic, not all that long after arriving in Canada. Far from making it big, he was buried in a pauper's grave. Whether this news contributed to my mother's own death, I cannot say, but she did appear to me to go downhill rapidly after receiving it.

So although my mother's sorry past doesn't wholly excuse the way she was to treat me, it does go some way to explain what was to follow, or at least puts it into some sort of context, and allows one to see and to understand how and why we tend to allow these cycles of misery and unnecessary suffering to continue. This book is not about fault and blame – it's about understanding.

The earliest memory that I have of my mother is also the most trau-matic. I must have been about six or seven years old, and was suffering from a chesty cough. The remedy my mother used for this particular ailment was a kaolin poultice, a porridge-like substance, spread on a cloth, and then applied to the chest. I don't understand why, but for the remedy to be effective the poultice had to be hot, but my mother must have misjudged the temperature, because it scalded me.

I screamed at her to take it off me, but this seemed to enrage her, and she just started pressing it down on me all the harder, all the time telling me to be quiet, it was supposed to be warm, and I was not to make such a fuss, it would make my cough better.

I was terrified, and just screamed louder and louder. What made it even more frightening was that this was my own mother who was hurting me, and I couldn't understand why.

What happened next I do not recall – I must have fallen asleep. The next thing that I remember is my mother screaming, and the doctor coming into the room.

"What have I done to my poor wee lassie?" my mother wailed. In spite of the pain that I was in, I felt so sorry for her. It had to be my fault that this had happened, and I wanted to do something, anything, to put it right, to stop her screaming and being upset. I just kept saying: "I'm sorry, I'm sorry!"

The doctor said nothing, but came over to examine me. He had to cut the poultice off – it had melted my skin and was stuck fast. The blisters on my chest were so huge that and they had to be burst open, and allowed to drain. I was afraid to move my arms, and just held them out in front of me.

The physical scars from my burns have remained with me for the whole of my life. I have seen them every day, but pretended to myself and to the rest of the world that they did not exist, that the whole scary episode had never taken place at all. The mental scars also have taken a long time to erase – the idea that, however badly my family treated me, it was somehow my fault, became a mind-set that it has taken until quite recently to dislodge.

I never mentioned the subject to my mother for as long as she lived, and she only began to allude to it once. I think that she was about to say how sorry she was about it, but I did not let her continue, and told her that I did not wish to talk about it. It wasn't important; it didn't bother me at all. But it did bother me, and I cannot believe that she did not realise that it must have bothered me. But my only concern at the time was to spare her any return of the upset I had apparently caused her that morning with the doctor. I could keep up any pretence and camouflage that would help to avoid that.

We thus were joined in a conspiracy of silence, hiding the secret trauma behind a mask of family respectability. These things didn't happen in nice families, only to other people's, and even then, we don't really want to know too much about it.

Another aspect of my family's treatment of me which, looked at impersonally, might possibly seem less traumatic than being burned, even relatively trivial perhaps, was her attitude, and that of my grandmother, towards my weight.

Now it is true that about the age of twelve or thirteen, I did start to put on a few pounds. But today, looking at photographs taken at the time, it seems barely noticeable – hardly even what you would expect of any normal healthy youngster at some stage or stages of growing up.

My mother began to make an issue of my size however, and said that I would need to have my clothes specially made-to-measure because I was (according to her) beginning to put the weight on, and what with my being unusually broad-shouldered, didn't look nice. My initial response was to eat all the more, but even then it hardly warranted these extreme measures. However, there was a secret reason for my mother's behaviour.

My father was a strict teetotaller, and had even given up cigarettes altogether. My mother loved smoking, but instead of asserting her right to do so if she wished, regardless of his views and opinions, she pretended to him that she only smoked a very occasional cigarette, when someone came to visit, for example.

As no-one in their right mind would have enjoyed paying a social visit to our house of their own free will, this didn't happen very often, so she had to work out other, more effective, wiles and stratagems.

Mrs Robertson was one of the dressmakers in the village, but as well as being an excellent seamstress, she had an even greater propensity for local gossip. She had a ferocious physiognomy, not a single tooth in her gums, and a giant hook nose, of which Cyrano de Bergerac himself would have been hugely proud. She was the perfect personification of my idea of what a wicked witch should look like, although I must admit that she was actually always quite nice to me when I was in her presence.

The main source of my fascination for her, and also the only reason for my mother's interest in her, was her incredible and quite superhuman ability to keep a lighted Woodbine constantly between her lips every minute of the day (and of the night, for all I know – I could well imagine her puffing away in her sleep).

Nothing and no-one whatsoever was allowed to interrupt or interfere with her ceaseless and blissful communion with nicotine. Certainly not conversation, as she could perform the two arts simultaneously with the greatest of ease, the Woodbine in her mouth sticking to the inside of her bottom lip, and waggling to the rhythm of her words, the ash growing miraculously longer and longer, until, eventually it could support its own weight no more, and fell helplessly down onto one of her chins.

An amber streak set out from the top of her lip, proceeded up the middle of her face, struck out boldly across her snow-white hair, only to disappear into obscurity somewhere around the crown of her head, clearly marking out the path that cigarette smoke had been habitually travelling during the previous fifty years or more.

Whenever I was getting any clothes made, my mother would take me round to Mrs Robertson's two or three times a week for fitting sessions, on account of my constantly changing shape and size. But my contribution to the evening's proceedings was over in a few seconds. Mrs Robertson would whip her tape from around her neck, measure whichever of my dimensions was supposed to have increased since our last visit, and that was it – I was surplus to requirements for the rest of the evening.

But I had served my purpose; I had provided my mother with her excuse and alibi for my father. Now she was free to settle back in one of the old grandfather chairs, take out a packet of twenty Bristol tipped, and smoke away to her heart's content for the next three or four hours, all the time gossiping away to the dressmaker, whilst the latter made a great play of being terribly busy, by dramatically flourishing her needle and thread to and fro through the air.

I was in torture. Forced to sit there with nothing to do, I felt myself being gradually asphyxiated amidst the swirling clouds of acrid smoke rapidly thickening around me. The open log fire hissed and wheezed contentedly, adding its own contribution to the polluted atmosphere. Now and then it would punctuate its ruminations with a regular dropping of ash into the hearth.

Mrs Robertson made it one of her strictest principles in life never to clean, sweep or polish her workplace, stoutly maintaining to anyone who would listen, that after the first ten years the dust never got any deeper.

Gazing round this cluttered, poky little room, pieces of thread littering the badly frayed carpet, and every visible surface piled high with clothes waiting to be either finished or mended, and topped up with odds and ends of assorted haberdashery, I could not for the life of me understand how my mother could appear so content to be here.

It was so unlike her own house, which was always clean and tidy, spick and span at all times, to the point of being clinical. The dressmaker's house was so diametrically different in kind to my mother's that I would have thought that it would have offended against her most basic principles to be seen even passing the door.

But thinking about it since, I have realised that, just like me spending as much of my time as possible out of doors, getting up to mischief either on my own or with my companions, and just like my father working away from home as long hours as he could, so my mother too was using these dressmaking sessions in order to effect her own escape.

With me by her side as her excuse, she too was managing to find a temporary parole from the rigid disciplinarian perfection that characterised our house. Publicly, she subscribed to it, as we all had to, because my father dictated that it should be so, but seemingly both of them, and certainly I for my part (I don't know about my brother and sister) found the constant perfection too much to bear all the time, and each of us in our own way had to find our own piece of regular, but short-lived, relief.

But it wasn't just the many long boring evenings spent in this way that upset me, nor the time spent in that choking unhealthy atmosphere that did the only damage. It was more that this remorselessly regular ritual only served to emphasise to me, and to indelibly imprint upon my mind, that I must be fat.

If it had merely been the case that I had to get my clothes made to measure, and not off-the-peg like other children, I may well not have noticed. But the fact that apparently so much time and trouble had necessarily to be expended in order to clothe me, seemed to indicate to me that I was indeed a nuisance to my mother, who could not in any way be at fault in the matter.

One particular memory now makes me realise that none of this nonsense was necessary in the first place. My mother had taken me to Mrs Robertson's house one evening to collect a new dress for me which she had just finished making. It was ghastly, and when I tried it on and saw myself in the mirror I had never seen anything quite so awful in all my life. In spite of both my mother and the dressmaker telling me how beautiful it was, I just burst into tears. I was inconsolable, and even my mother must have sensed the depth of my misery and desolation, for, when we got home, she promised that she would buy me a new skirt and blouse for my birthday the following week.

This she did, and I was duly glad and grateful. But this only went to show that I could have had my clothes bought for me ready-made and off-the-peg all along – just like other children in other normal families did all the time. And if this wasn't bad enough she decided that I needed a light corset. She made me wear it to school – much to my embarrassment, in case anybody would find out – saying that it would give me a nicer shape like Elsie.

I never did actually have a weight problem, but other people certainly gave me one. If my mother first planted the seed of the problem in my mind, then it was my grandmother who fed and watered it, nurtured it and brought it to full bloom. It was about the same time (when I was about twelve or thirteen years old) that my grandparents, who were retired, came to live in Lochwinnoch. They were English, and I loved listening to their Lancashire accents. My father had been born down south, and had come to Scotland aged 10 when his parents had moved to Glasgow for the first time. They had moved back to England with one of their sons when they retired, leaving the rest of their family settled in Scotland.

I had used to enjoy visiting them at their smallholding and market garden overlooking the River Clyde. I was in paradise, wandering through the greenhouses with their unforgettable fragrant aroma of fruit and flowers. That was where Adam, my grandfather, was invariably to be found, kneeling in his leather-patched trousers amongst his beloved creations. A strict teetotaller, he was not a churchgoer, but a God-fearing, decent, good-living man, who seemed in perfect harmony with the work that he did, and whose favourite quotation from the Bible was 'The earth is the Lord's, and the fullness thereof.'

The kitchen was my grandmother's domain. Surrounded by good food and the smells of home cooking, Martha's day was a constant round of roasting chickens, baking bread, boiling soups, and preserving windfall fruit and excess vegetables by making jams, chutneys and pickles – all from the Garden of Eden, for Eden was Martha's maiden name.

The house seemed to overflow with the best of everything that the earth could offer, and man could lovingly cultivate. Nothing was ever wasted, even apparent dross was put to use, and added to the chicken feed.

Resplendent and reigning supreme in her own kingdom, she was plumply confident in everything she did. I used to watch fascinated as a fold of fat beneath her arm, between her shoulder and her elbow, flapped gaily to and fro as determinedly she beat the eggs or kneaded the dough.

I loved being in that house – I felt safe, snug and secure. I always looked forward to the times when they said that the roads were too bad, or whatever, to get back to Lochwinnoch that day, and that I would have to stay overnight. What joy to be tucked up warm in that great brass bedstead, knowing that it was cold outside the recessed windows, but that the long red velvet curtains would be standing guard all night, to make sure that it stayed out there.

Of my grandmother in the past, then, fond memories indeed. But when she came to live in Lochwinnoch, it seemed to me that, when no other grown-up was around, either she was a changed woman, or that her attitude towards me had changed completely. If the latter was the case, I wonder whether it might be because I was then about thirteen years old – around about the same age at which, many years before, her own daughter Elsie (after whom my sister was named) had died. Perhaps I reminded her of Elsie, and she unconsciously resented the fact that her daughter had died, and I was still alive.

Every day after school I was expected to do her shopping before I could get out to play with my friends. She would make out a list, and one day it included some lemons.

At that time there were no self-service shops in Lochwinnoch, and as I ran down the street I would be praying to myself that there would not be a long queue to delay me. I would give the list to the woman behind the counter, and she would make up the order.

On that particular day, the lemons were too green for my grandmother. But the way she went on about it, you would have thought that it was my fault, whereas she knew that it was the shop assistant who had chosen them. But that didn't seem to matter to my gran, and desperate as I was to get out to play, I had to go back to the shop, and stand in another long queue. Only this time it was even worse, because I was so embarrassed having to tell the lady in the shop that if she didn't have any riper lemons, I was to get her money back.

When she was in one of her moods, she kept me hanging around, making her coffee. I could only leave when she said so. But the worse she was to me, the nicer I was to her. On some other days, however, she would ask if I would like a glass of lemonade before I went to the shops. This was her all the time – I never knew what to expect. Sometimes she even refused to let me into the house when I visited her unexpectedly to see how she was. I heard her saying to my grandfather: "Tell her we're not having visitors today, and shut that door!"

And it wasn't long before she homed in on my weight. One time, my parents took a short holiday away together, as my grandparents had offered to look after my brother and sister and me.

Every Saturday it was a regular ritual for the three of us to go to the local sweetshop, and each buy sixpence-worth of different kinds. We would then go back home and gleefully sit down around the kitchen table to share them all out, carefully counting out each one, so that we would all end up with an assortment.

On this occasion however, when we came back to enact our weekly ceremony at my grandmother's house, she took charge. Seeing that the sweets did not divide up equally, and that there were two left over, her shiny red fat hand swooped upon the two remaining sweets, snatched them up and thrust one each in the direction of Gordon and Elsie.

"You don't need any extras!" my Gran mocked me. "You're too fat already!"

What made it worse for me was the fact that Gordon could hardly stop himself laughing and pointing at me.

For our tea on Saturdays we three children were always treated to our favourite sausages and chips – and I thought that my parents' absence that weekend would not be allowed to interfere with our usual routine.

I should have known better. From the sweetie-sharing incident that morning, I should have been able to see which way the wind was blowing. That evening as we were about to eat, my grandmother stood four-square in front of the kitchen stove, arms akimbo, shoulders straight, and smugly informed me in her tight- lipped way, "There's no chips for you, my lady, just sausage! You're ugly and fat enough as it is, you don't need any encouragement!"

Her behaviour towards me was never consistent, for there were other times, when she'd been baking for instance, when she would coax me to eat, even when I wasn't hungry, and to me that was very confusing.

Many years later, I learned that at this time my grandmother had been told by her doctor in no uncertain terms that she was unhealthily overweight, and that she had no choice but to under go a strict diet. She hated this, because she loved her grub! And isn't it strange how common it is for people to seek enthusiastically to inflict their own suffering onto others?

That night as I was getting ready for bed, I went to hide one of my most treasured and private possessions, a tin of Nivea cream for my face. I was just tucking it into the toe of one of my shoes in the cupboard, so that no one would know that I had it, when my grandmother silently entered the room and with a determined look, asked: "What are you doing?"

I got such a fright, I jumped back.

"Nothing, Granny," I replied.

"I'll nothing you!" She nudged past me, lifted up my shoes, and out fell the tin of Nivea. Looking at it scornfully, she sneered, "You'll have no need for this, my girl. It'll take a lot more than Nivea cream to make you beautiful. You're not as nice as your sister. Beauty creams won't do any good for ugly fat elephants."

Thrusting the offending tin into her apron pocket, she stalked triumphantly out of the door.

She was the first person to make remarks directly to me about my weight. They might be considered just foolish words, I never realised then the devastating impact that they were to have upon my life.

That night I cried myself asleep under the blankets, trying my hardest to muffle the sound, so that no one would discover my misery, convinced that this would be held against me as well, and make matters even worse than they were already. We children were allowed to cry (as long as we didn't make a meal of it) if we had grazed our knee, for instance. You can see a wound, but feelings and emotions are invisible, and therefore so far as my family was concerned, they didn't exist – they weren't allowed to exist.

When my parents got back from their holiday, I remember telling my mother what my gran had said, and then her telling my father. He had already been told about the times she had not let me into the house. Now standing quietly in the background, I was hoping for his support. But again he said nothing, because that was *his* mother. When you don't get support, and you are not allowed to express how you feel, you belittle those feelings. But I in turn, later on in life, wouldn't allow anyone to say anything about him, because he was my father.

My grandmother was a strong-willed, intolerant woman, devoid of humour, who behaved at times with a childish cruelty, and who seemed to enjoy mocking other people, especially those who had the cheek to disagree with her.

On several occasions I remember her boasting that she didn't believe in smacking a child. But she forgot that a verbal lashing was just as bad as a physical blow – mostly you never forget the cruel things that people say to you. They are simply put to the back of your mind, gone, but not forgotten. Or as that well-known song goes: "When it's too painful to remember, we simply choose to forget." I can look back now, and remember 'the way we were'.

My grandmother's reference to my sister, comparing me with her to my disadvantage, was to be a recurrent theme in my life for many years to come. There was even an echo of it quite recently, which shows how it passed into and became part of our family mythology.

There was an old friend of my mother whom the family knew well and called aunt. Murdoch and I took her out to dinner some years ago, which gave them the opportunity to meet, and us all the chance to celebrate her recent birthday. In the midst of the conversation, and quite out of the blue, leaning over the table and in a confidential tone, she remarked to Murdoch, "But, of course, you know, if you'd seen Lilian's sister Elsie first, you'd never have looked at Lilian in the first place!"

This incident shows how far I still had to travel along the road to radical recovery, when I remember that my only reaction at that time was to smile sweetly and pour myself another glass of wine! I can see clearly now, and realise that my aunt, like my grandmother with her weight problem, was trying to rid herself of her inferiority complex, by seeking to transfer it on to me.

Not all my aunts were like this. There was one who seemed to sense that I was unhappy, and that was my Aunt Jessie. She always gave me a lot of praise, was interested in how I was getting on, and cared about whether I was happy or not. She was fat, but confident with it. Nobody would have dared to mention her size in front of her, and I liked her for this. She once invited me to her house in Glasgow for the weekend, as her daughter Doreen was taking part in a ballet performance. This was the first time that I had been away from home on my own, and I had such fun, that I can still remember it today.

My family's contrasting attitudes towards Elsie and myself came into focus most clearly when we were in our later teens, when we first went out to work, and at the time of the beauty contest.

When she left school, my sister went to work for Mrs McGilchrist, who owned one of the local hairdressing salons. Elsie's new employer, who soon became a family friend, firmly believed that it was good for her business if she and the girls in the shop were all well made-up, with their hair fashionably cut, and even tinted.

So, with Mrs McGilchrist to back her up, if necessary, Elsie did not encounter the same persistent opposition from our father to her cosmetic experimentation as I had done. In fact it was most noticeable to me that she encountered no opposition at all.

Elsie had the freedom (and the money from her tips) to buy all the latest fashionable and expensive clothes and make-up, and I felt quite honoured when she let me borrow anything of hers, the likes of which I could never afford out of my pocket money. She gave me the impression of feeling a cut above me, she never seemed to notice my having less than she did, and the rest of my family just turned a blind eye.

It was Mrs McGilchrist who suggested that my sister should enter a beauty contest that was being held at that time in Glasgow, and this idea caused a great stir of excitement throughout the family.

A photographer was summoned to the house to take pictures of Elsie, who was looking slender in her beautiful new dress. Sitting alone and unnoticed, set apart from all the attention which she was receiving as she stood gracefully posed in the limelight of the camera's flash-lamp, I was now even more convinced than ever that the thinner you were the more beautiful and attractive to other people you were as well. Now I thought that I would have to start dieting, and because I must be ugly as well, I would camouflage my face with make-up.

When I first left school my father had arranged for me to get a job working behind the shop counter of Mr Ross the chemist. It seemed only natural that as I was supposed to be selling, even advising, women about cosmetics, I should get to know a bit about them. So I tried one or two of the samples available, the brightest lipstick, I remember it was called 'Riding Hood Red', and the most vivid blue eye shadow. It wouldn't have been tolerated at home for an instant, but this was different, I was out in the world. Or so I thought.

Suddenly the shop doorbell tinkled, and there stood my father, radiating an icy rage that petrified me. "Take that paint off your face this instant! I'll speak to you at home at lunchtime."

After this, my father made a point of calling on his old friend Mr Ross for a regular twice a week chat in the back shop. The old chemist was nearing retirement, and wanted me to study pharmacy, perhaps with the unspoken intention of my eventually taking over from him, but I knew that my father's visits were not just to do with concern for the future of Mr Ross's business, or of my prospective career. He was merely taking every available opportunity to keep an eye on me as well.

Life and work in the shop became very oppressive for me. Because the old chemist was such a good friend of my father, I felt that they were two spies in league together against me, one in my very midst, observing my every movement, ensuring that I made no unauthorised exit from my open prison, the other acting as back-up, vigilantly patrolling the village streets, alert and ready to effect my instant recapture, should I ever make so bold as to break out from captivity.

Had I been more self-confident and self-assertive I could have walked out of that situation, or changed it to one more to my satisfaction at any time, but instead of facing up to the situation head-on, and dealing with it in a direct and straightforward manner, my escape was actually effected by a combination of guile and good fortune.

Not long afterwards Mr Ross took leave of absence due to ill health, and I took advantage of this period of uncertainty about the future of the business to enrol for evening classes in shorthand, typing and English. I thought that this would meet with the approval of my father (it did – he always used to say that education was a wonderful thing) but really it was something that at that time I genuinely wanted to try, and it proved quite enjoyable.

But the real bonus was that it got me out of the house three evenings a week, and it actually turned out to be even better than that. One of the new friends I made at the evening classes was a girl called Oonah Moncrieff, who told me that there was a secretarial job vacant where she worked at Neilson & Barclay Ltd, a small engineering company in Johnstone, Renfrewshire. I went for the interview. The managing director dictated a letter for me to take down in shorthand, and then timed how long it took me to type out. Soon after, I was told there and then that the job was mine.

It turned out that Oonah had been using a bit of guile herself, and had been somewhat economical with the truth. Yes, there had been a job going – the one that I was now doing. What she had omitted to tell me was that she herself had already handed in her notice, which meant that I would shortly have to be doing both hers and mine. The way I managed it was that my father had bought me a second-hand typewriter, and I could take work home when necessary. Fortunately things worked out perfectly, and I spent almost three years at Neilson & Barclay, enjoying every minute of it.

The best bit of all was that I was now working all day every weekday away from the house, away from Lochwinnoch, and, most important out from under my father's close inspection. Admittedly it was only a half-hour's bus ride away, but judging by the great feeling of freedom and independence it afforded me, I could have been on the other side of the world.

I milked this opportunity dry. On Mondays, Tuesdays and Thursdays I could quite easily have had the time to return home from work for my tea, before setting off afterwards for my evening classes. But in order to gain the absolute maximum time away from the house, I pretended otherwise to my parents, went without my tea, and stayed on the bus from Johnstone to Kilbirnie when it passed through Lochwinnoch.

I also had another secret that nobody knew about. Forgoing my tea was not the privation that it might seem; in fact it suited me fine. For by this time it had clicked with me that I was fat, and fat was ugly. I would never have been allowed to diet at home in the severe and thorough way that I was now doing, but now, out of sight and out of mind for so much of the time, I was free to continue to starve myself in my own silent and defiant way, in a lonesome, valiant attempt to gain approval from my family, and from the world at large.

By now I had got all my shorthand typing and English language certificates from night school and was a qualified shorthand typist. I thought I would spread my wings, and try to get better job, which would take me even more out into the world. So having successfully applied for a vacancy, I joined India Tyres in Inchinnan, between Paisley and Glasgow.

This was supposed to be a secretarial job, but when I arrived on my first day, they decided that they were so short-staffed in the ledger department that I would be more useful there.

I just smiled and agreed, but when I was escorted to my new workplace on my first morning and opened the door, I was completely and utterly thrown. There were about thirty women all scurrying about, up to their eyes in work, so nobody had enough time to sit down and show me what was required. Most of the time I wasn't sure what I was doing, but tried to struggle on unaided, what with being shy with strange people, and frightened to ask too many questions in case they thought that I was stupid.

I soon began to withdraw. It was too big a challenge to progress at work – I just wanted to escape. I wished that I was married – that would take me out of India Tyres, and also out of the family home. And that's exactly what I did.

The first bright spark that I had ever shown in gaining secretarial qualifications, that burning ambition to do well was just like a candle quickly snuffed out. From then on, for the next twenty-five years or so, until I met Murdoch, my life was to become a series of beginnings and endings – all the major choices and decisions I made were all for the wrong reasons. I never felt that I belonged in any place, or with anyone, and my heart was never in anything. I was so mixed up and so lost at one point that often I said to myself: "I want to go home. But I don't know where home is."

Within a year, when I was nineteen years old, and engaged to be married, I discovered that I was pregnant. I was happy about this, because it would mean that I could leave home, and the thought of me becoming a parent delighted me, but I was worried about how I was to tell my mother. She began to notice that I was becoming increasingly withdrawn, and would ask me what was wrong. Each time I would insist that there was nothing wrong, I was just tired.

A few nights later, I had deliberately stayed out late, so that everybody would be in bed by the time I got in. But my mother had stayed up, and was in the kitchen making coffee.

When she had poured me a cup, we both sat down at the table. She broached the subject again, but this time her voice had dropped, and her tone was soft and gentle.

"Lilian, you can tell me anything – I won't be annoyed, everything will be all right."

I burst out crying, and told her what was wrong, and at that she jumped up, thumping her hand on the table.

"You dirty little bitch! How could you? How dare you?" she raged.

Then she put all the lights in the house on, marched upstairs to wake my father, and in doing so succeeded also in rousing the whole household. As she announced the news, her main concern was not for me, but for herself. She was anxious that everybody should see her in a good light as a good mother who had done her best to bring me up properly, and that she was in no way responsible for my turning out the way I had. It was nothing to do with her. I had let her and the rest of my family down. She would not or could not accept any blame herself.

As a punishment, she refused to pay for my wedding outfit. She said, "If you want it, you'll need to work for it yourself." I had to take on an extra Saturday job and save up the money myself. But although my fiancé and I did save as much as we could, she still insisted upon choosing the outfit herself, and I hated it.

This incident, together with a combination of many others, resulted in my firm conviction that I could never trust anybody's word, and that I could only rely upon myself. I would do things my way.

I did look after myself during pregnancy, but after my son John was born, it was back to the strictest of diets. I now got by on one small meal a day. After a while I found that I had lost quite a bit of weight, and this began to make me think that my appearance must have improved. I was now well and truly on the slippery slope.

My dieting continued to get inexorably worse as time went on. It rapidly became an obsession. As far as food was concerned, it was as though I had taken religious vows of self-denial. I remember once someone bought me a box of chocolates, which I was desperate to eat, but I couldn't even allow myself one. If someone had tried to make me, I would have been trembling with fear. I was scared to eat anything at all over and above my meagre rations. Just one chocolate would have meant that I would have lost control and scoffed the lot – just the same way as, if I had taken a glass of whisky, I would have drunk the whole bottle.

In those days no-one spoke of *anorexia nervosa* – I don't know if the term had even been invented – it certainly wasn't something that I knew about then. Twiggy and Jean Shrimpton were the fashionable photographic models of the time, so slimness, even thinness, were very much in vogue, as they are still today of course, but at least there is now more general awareness about the pain and the problems that can lurk behind the smiling façade.

Some of the media accuse modelling agencies of causing anorexia by exploiting the skinny look, but they say they are only providing what the public wants. Some magazines are trying to change this by using models with a more rounded figure. Anorexia is different from strict dieting. Most people on a strict diet will use portion-control, still getting their essential nutrients. True anorexia, on the other hand, is life threatening. I believe that only people who have been psychologically damaged become self-harmers.

Once I remember, after I had got married and had left home, my mother had to go into hospital. After visiting her one afternoon, I went back to the house with my father. Quite out of the blue, and most unexpectedly, he suggested that he cook us both a meal. Perhaps the word 'suggest' gives the wrong impression, because my father's suggestion was the same as any other person's command. Before I had time to think of a reason or an excuse why I could not stay, he had already put some pieces of chicken breast into the oven, and started to peel the potatoes to make chips. I was in agony. On the one hand I was starving; on the other, I knew that I could not, and would not eat.

They say that you can lead a horse to water, but you cannot force it to drink. By this time, this was certainly true of myself and food. Unfortunately, whereas if it had been anybody other than my father, I could have politely made it perfectly plain that for whatever reason, it was not possible for me to stay to eat, with my father I was unable to assert myself openly and directly. As so often before, I had to resort to more guileful and devious means.

For once, luck was on my side. At the very moment that he put the plate of chicken, chips and salad down in front of me, the telephone started to ring in the hall, and he left the room to answer it. I hadn't a moment to lose. As quick as lightning, I grabbed two paper serviettes, and in them deftly wrapped everything from my plate, save for a solitary lettuce leaf and a slice of tomato. That much I could tolerate, but no more, the rest I whisked into my handbag to dispose of later. Just at that very instant, my father came back into the room.

As he gazed at my empty plate (by this time I was munching contentedly on the lettuce leaf), his eyes opened wide in amazement and disbelief. "By God!" he said. "That was quick! I thought you said you'd lost your appetite. I see you've found a horse's instead!"

My descent into the abyss was not evenly spaced, some periods of my life were better than others, sometimes my dieting was more severe, and at others it was less.

But predominantly, my governing preoccupation was that of food, or more exactly how I could best avoid consuming any.

During one of my dry spells when I was attending *AA* meetings, I was chatting to another member, and telling them a bit about my starvation diet. He said to me in a puzzled tone: "Why can't you just eat normally like everybody else?"

Quick as a flash I replied: "Why can't you just *drink* normally like everybody else?"

At one stage things had become so bad that my hair actually stopped growing, and clumps of it were falling out. Not surprisingly, I was also feeling quite unwell and constantly lethargic, so eventually made an appointment to see the doctor. I deliberately told him nothing about my dieting, and he didn't mention anything about my weight either. Instead he asked me a few general questions, and wrote me out a prescription for some vitamin pills. I did get these from the chemist, but I had to force myself to take them, terrified lest they might contain even just a few extra calories, and make me put on some more unwanted weight. And I used to inspect every brand of face cream in order to try to find the least enriched and oily one, as I was totally convinced that any excess would soak through my skin and make my face and neck fatter.

The daily rations that I now allowed myself consisted of a tiny boiled egg and a small cup of unsweetened black coffee for breakfast, nothing at all during the day apart from more black coffee, and one boiled potato accompanied by a minute serving of one or two other vegetables in the evening. Once I had adopted this routine, it rapidly became an unalterable habit, one that it would have upset me deeply to alter in a single detail, even for one day.

My weight dropped to six stone two pounds, but that was me dressed in my fleecy-lined anorak, loose baggy trousers, a couple of sweaters and knee-length fur-lined boots, a mode of attire that also served to disguise from the world at large how unhealthily thin I was really becoming. However, if anyone did chance to mention that I was looking a bit under-weight, far from taking this as a warning, it actually pleased me, and spurred me on to even greater efforts.

It would have been quite bad enough if my anorexia had been the total extent of my problems – in fact, it was barely even half of them. Such an iron grip kept on my food intake over so many years of my life would not have been possible without some means of escape being available whenever it was unconsciously required. And just as the dieting I needed to escape from was extreme, it was probably inevitable that the refuge to which I escaped was equally extreme. I found alcohol, and when I drank, I allowed myself to eat.

Not that I started off drinking alcoholically, far from it. While I was young, my parents were both teetotal (they thought that it was morally and socially correct not to drink). My father had in turn inherited this attitude from his parents, who had both been stalwart members of the temperance movement. So as a youngster I grew up just naturally accepting that drink was wrong, without ever questioning whether this supposition was correct or not. It wasn't until I got older and left home that I started kicking back against this.

After I got married, I was moving in a different circle of friends, who *did* drink as a matter of routine at weekends, although none of them alcoholically. I came to accept that it was quite natural and normal for people (including myself) to have a drink on a Saturday night. I have heard people in *AA* describe how their first drink opened up a brave new world for them, a marvellous liberating experience. Well, yes, it was for me too, but not just because of the alcohol. Although I would not have admitted it to anybody at the time, not even to myself, just one drink (although two were better) relaxed the tight iron grip I was exerting over the real Lilian imprisoned deep inside me, desperately trying to get out, and lo and behold I started to eat!

All right, it was only a few peanuts, or maybe a sandwich, but you've got to remember, that was a feast for me. And after the third or fourth drink, which was about as much as any of us did drink at that time, I was well into my stride in the eating stakes, and I could enjoy a late-night supper along with the rest of the company, with neither a thought nor a qualm. But I would have to go without anything at all the next day to compensate, and, full of guilt, it would be back to the diet as usual on the Monday.

This comparatively gentle game of seesaw continued in much the same pattern for some time, but it was not long before the downswings increased in length. The few drinks on Saturday night became a few drinks on Friday evening as well, then finally they spread to include Sunday night, so that, although I was not drinking during the day, the whole weekend was beginning to be focused entirely upon, and dominated by, the idea of alcohol.

Essentially, it was not only my appetite for drink that was increasing; it was also my appetite for food, and escape from the restricting confines of my self-imposed semi-starvation regime. Escape, too, from the bizarre, complex structure of repression and denial that, in my head, my whole life and existence had increasingly developed into.

Two selves within me were incompatible. My true self, whom I barely knew, a stranger passed from time to time, recognised briefly without knowing who it was, then once again forgotten. And the other one, the one that I created. The self I thought I had to be, the self I sometimes thought that I desired to be. But it was this false self that kept going on benders. I had to find my real identity.

So things got worse – and worse, and worse. It is hardly surprising that the weekend drinking began from time to time to drift into benders. With benders came bouts of depression of increasing severity, probably due to the fact that I despised how I was behaving, could not understand why I was doing it, and even less did I think I was able to do anything to stop it.

It felt as though I was chained to three or four different treadmills all at the same time. All these treadmills were carrying me helplessly, inevitably towards a deep yawning chasm opening up before me, in which lay only disaster, utter despair, and a sense of detachment from the real world and from my own true self. I thought it was hopeless. I could see no way out of my predicament, no possible avenue of escape.

Chapter Four
Recovery Through Discovery

My heart leaps up when I behold
A rainbow in the sky:
So was it when my life began;
So is it now I am a man;
So be it when I shall grow old.
Or let me die!
The Child is father of the Man;
And I could wish my days to be
Bound each to each by natural piety.

William Wordsworth

ABOUT two years before I met Murdoch, my mother died. She died alone in the house while my father was out doing the daily shopping. In the months leading up to her death she had looked terrible – like me coming off a bender. Every day she was continually shaking, and found it difficult to walk unaided, although this was nothing to do with old age.

For at least 25 years my mother had become reliant upon and mis-used prescribed drugs. These were nerve tablets, anti-depressants and sleeping pills. She had first been prescribed them by her GP to help her through a time of family upset, and quite simply never got off them.

For the first fifteen years or so, nobody in the family bothered about it – it was only in the last ten years before her death aged 69 that the dete-rioration really set in. By the end, she had lost the will to live, and told me often that she prayed to die. Sometimes she would ask me: "Why do I feel as bad as this, when I've done nothing wrong?" One time I replied: "Mum, because you've done nothing about sorting out what is wrong, why you started taking all these pills in the first place."

She wasn't pleased about me saying this. She looked at me in disgust. "What do you know about it?" was all that she said.

At first, it was just the nerve tablets – a mild dose, one three times a day. Then it gradually progressed – she moved on to anti-depressants as well, and before too long, stronger doses and sleeping pills were added. They had just become repeat prescriptions, which she would order before she had run out, and over the years built up a hidden surplus hoard 'just in case she needed them' – in exactly the same way as many alcoholics do with their booze. This allowed her to take extra pills when she felt like it, without anybody realising what was going on.

I only discovered this by chance during one of her really bad times. She was in her bed, and had asked me to fetch her a packet of cigarettes from her handbag in the hall cupboard, and open the window and help her over to it so that she could blow the smoke out, and avoid my father finding out.

Unfortunately, there were two handbags in the cupboard – and I opened the wrong one! Stuffed inside were dozens of packs of tablets of various kinds, some full, some half-empty.

I couldn't believe what I was seeing, and, confused, I took the bag through to my mother and emptied it out on the bed. "Mum, what are all these for?" I began to ask, but she was angry at being found out, and refused to speak about it, telling me that it was none of my business.

I started to tell my father about this, but before I could finish what I wanted to say, he drew up his head indignantly, giving the appearance of looking down his nose at me. "Your mother's pills have been prescribed by the doctor. Are you trying to tell me that you know better than him?" He refused to allow any further discussion.

And that was my family all the time – whenever there was something wrong that they didn't understand or try to understand, they distanced themselves, giving an air of rising above such matters. They felt superior to all that, and left me (and probably my mother) feeling inferior.

Not long after that, the family doctor had arranged for someone from Dykebar psychiatric hospital in Paisley to visit the house to make an assessment of my mother's condition. We were all very shocked – the words 'psychiatric hospital' had never figured in our family vocabulary before.

I went over the next day to find out how she had got on. My father was upset, (as I was), and told me in a hushed voice: "The very worst has happened. Your mother is going to be admitted into Dykebar tomorrow. She is suffering from depression."

The following afternoon I went to visit her. I found her in the patients' day room, looking lost. After a cup of coffee, she told me that she had been speaking to other patients earlier in the day – apparently some of them were alcoholics in to 'dry out', and this had shocked her. "What a cheek!" she said, "putting me in the same ward as bloody alkies!"

I didn't say anything – I was just as confused as she was – but it made me think.

And little did I know then, that some years later I too would be hospitalised - but I would be one of the "bloody alkies"!

Thinking back over the years, I never really knew my mother at all. Her identity or personality as an individual had evaporated a long time before, and all that remained was an empty shell. The only thing I knew about my mother was that she liked her coffee made with all milk, not water.

The one sad memory she left me was of a disturbed woman who never wanted to join in anything going on around her. When the family decided to have a day out, my mother would usually say: "You all go – I'll just stay at home." And sometimes when we got home, she would be just sitting pensively in her chair.

Our family dealt with this simply by urging her to 'cheer up', but she always seemed to be on the outside looking in. It must have appeared to me and others then as if she just didn't want to go out – that was her choice. But at other times she was so sad looking, although she tried to hide it.

She was probably afraid to admit to my father that she was unhappy – what could she be unhappy about, would have been my father's reaction, there's nothing wrong in here, looking round the lovely house and landscaped garden that he had provided her with.

My father always pooh-poohed whenever she tried to talk about her lost childhood, and although she told me bits and pieces throughout my teenage years, I said nothing, and changed the subject. At that time, I didn't think parents had problems, and would have been embarrassed to have witnessed a show of emotion. The fact that nobody would really listen to what she wanted to say must have increased her sense of sadness and loneliness still further.

And at times I was just the same.

At a time of affluence in my life, when the people around me thought that I should be happy, my then partner had a cabin cruiser, and he and my daughter and some friends would have great fun together on it. I would never join in, and one day on the way home my daughter said to me: "Mum, you don't appreciate the simple things in life!" And out came the words: "I can't reach them." I often had the sense of being on the outside looking in, as if there was a sheet of glass separating me from the real world.

It was often said to me at different times in my life that I would never be happy – no matter how much I had, there was still no pleasing me. I was also said by some to be moody. I was, but it wasn't what they were thinking. There was a part of the real me missing, I wasn't a whole person, but at that time I did not understand this. I had almost everything that money could buy, but I didn't have myself, I couldn't reach the real me. And until I found myself, I now know that I could never have been happy.

My mother's condition and mine shared the same cause – our childhood experiences – and the effects differed only in our particular drug of choice. In fact, my mother was a socially acceptable drug addict. But not everyone who has had a less than happy childhood turns to drink or drugs. Everybody is different. Some people actually respond positively, with an "I'll show you!" attitude, but that doesn't mean that they are really happy inside or at peace with themselves.

The one legacy my mother left me (and it was the only one!) was her obsessive cleaning. My whole house had to be hoovered, dusted and polished day in and day out, and felt I had to do a laundry and iron it every day as well.

When I had my children, I behaved the same as my mother, made the same big mistakes, and never gave them the time and attention that they needed, because I couldn't allow anything to interrupt my routine.

I absorbed everything that I saw my mother doing like a sponge does water, and was later to repeat the pattern for most of my adult life. My life wasn't my own, and in not being able to live the way I wanted, I never felt free and was always troubled. And with these levels of stress, something's got to give.

Naturally, all the family was very upset at my mother's death. After the initial shock it was decided that my sister Elsie would come over from Australia for the funeral. Arriving in Scotland at about 6pm on the evening before the funeral, my father, brother Gordon and his wife went to the airport to meet her. Later the same evening I telephoned her at my father's house, saying that I would drive up from Ayr to Lochwinnoch early the following morning, so that we would have the chance of a chat before leaving for the crematorium. But things didn't work out as I had imagined.

When I arrived the next day, everyone was drinking coffee, so I joined them. I sat down on the settee next to my sister-in-law, and suddenly caught sight of a very familiar pair of earrings that she was wearing. On many an occasion in the past I had admired them in my mother's jewellery box.

My father and brother must have noticed me looking dumbstruck, for my father made an excuse to disappear into the kitchen, leaving my brother to hesitantly start attempting an explanation: "Seeing that you were not here last night, your father decided to sort out all our mother's jewellery, and get that job out of the way before the funeral."

I thought this was strange, because they had known that I was going over earlier than need be that morning – so what had been the rush? There had obviously been a secret collaboration here.

After all, I was the elder sister, and surely I should have been in-cluded – in fact I should probably have had first choice. What was worse, even friends of my mother had been allocated the pieces of jew-ellery that my family thought they would have liked, and I was merely handed what was left.

My only outward reaction at the time was to smile and say: "thank you very much". But really I was angry and very upset, although my true feelings were quickly suppressed. Thinking that you can't say anything at this sad time (not that I would have anyway), by now my head was spinning.

For the time being, I put this incident out of my head. I would be having a drink after the funeral – and when I drink, I eat, so in spite of this mixture of sadness and gladness there was something to look forward to!

After the cremation, all family and friends were invited out for a light meal, and afterwards, if they wished, back to the house for a drink. Although neither my mother nor my father was a regular drinker, there was always a plentiful and varied stock of liquor in the house that had been given to them as presents in the past.

I've mentioned before that my grandparents were strictly teetotal, and wouldn't allow alcohol into their house at all. And my grandmother would not have approved if she had thought that her son had any in his. When my brother and sister and I were very young, this was indeed the case. As we got into our teens however, on special occasions like New Year for instance, I remember my parents taking a sherry, and my being allowed a very small glass of Babycham, provided that my grandparents or any of our other close relations weren't visiting us at the time, of course!

My father kept up this façade, not only in front of his mother, but in front of his brothers as well. It wasn't until a few years after my grandmother's death that he began to allow himself a bit more freedom, and to be coaxed into enjoying a sherry in the lounge bar of a hotel whilst ordering his meal.

But as time went on this became quite a regular thing. Towards the end of his life, when he and my mother went out to visit my sister and her husband in Australia, they would enjoy a large glass of brandy vino *every* night after their meal. My mother would be telling me this when they returned, quite surprised that my father actually seemed to be enjoying it, but he would always change the subject if this ever came up in conversation when he was present.

The December after my mother died, my father went back out to Australia on his own. When he telephoned to wish me a happy Christmas, he sounded quite squiffy. "We've had a wonderful day!" he proclaimed. "We've been drinking champagne since lunchtime!"

I was taken aback on hearing this, but I can work it all out now.

He no longer had to keep up his guise in front of my mother, and with my not being there, he did not need to keep up appearances in front of me. My sister Elsie and her husband Ian had always enjoyed a drink quite openly, whether my father was there or not. They didn't need his approval. And their daughter Lesley-Ann was allowed to join them once she was old enough. So on this occasion he was in the midst of his family and their friends who were all enjoying a drink. So what was unusual about that?

The unusual thing was that he had to wait until he was eighty years old before he started to allow his mask to slip. Everybody in Lochwinnoch who knew my father was under the impression that he was strictly teetotal, but in Australia, where none of my sister and brother-in-law's friends knew him, he could live the way he really wanted, without exciting any comment and possibly losing face.

He obviously enjoyed this new-found freedom so much, that as soon as he returned from his first solo trip to Australia, he immediately booked up his flight for a return visit. He died before he could make it, but I know what he meant when he told me that he 'he still had a lot of living to do'. Sadly, it was later than he thought.

Much earlier in my life, whenever we were at family gatherings, I behaved in the same way with my father as he had with his mother – I never took a drink when he was around. As I got older, I got more daring – provided that there was other company around. I thought that it would have annoyed and embarrassed him if he saw me enjoying a drink.

Now, at my mother's funeral, my father had one sherry, but I would have liked more – and had the impression that some of the other guests would too. But I couldn't say this out loud in front of him without a very good excuse. So I got up and went into the kitchen, and began to play 'mother'. Some of the others followed, and I asked one of them to go and ask how many would like another drink, and who would prefer tea or coffee. Behind the scenes now, I have two or three large ones.

I see now where most of my life has been a kickback. Lounge bars never suited me, because that's what my parents did. I wanted attention, and the places that made me feel good, where I could feel superior, were honky-tonk bars and jazz clubs. Chewing gum, with the flashiest earrings, the longest cigarette in a holder, I wanted to be free. I wanted to live on the wild side, or so I thought.

I acted the clown, and people treated me accordingly. But I was to discover later that I wasn't so much of a fool after all.

I had one or two large ones in the kitchen while serving the rest of the family, but there was such confusion going on in my head, I was soon glad to get back to my own house and have a few more drinks there. Numbed, I just wanted to go to sleep.

The next morning, however, as soon as I awoke, the sadness was magnified, and the gladness replaced by remorse. As I tried to lift my head up from the pillow, dread had set in, and I didn't know how I was going to get through the day without another drink to stop my mind racing.

I came down to the kitchen and went to the cupboard for a drink. Why was I feeling as bad as this? Other people had probably had as much as me to drink the previous evening, but they would be having tea or coffee this morning, not more alcohol. What was so different about me?

This drinking went on for about a week. At times like this I would never go out of the house, as I could telephone my order for what I needed to drink, and it would be delivered. I would just sit in the house, not saying anything to anybody, just staring in front of me, drinking, sleeping and crying, and driving my daughter crazy with worry. It felt like a circling of mental energy, never going anywhere or coming to any conclusions. It was sheer hell for me, and for everybody around me.

When I finally got off the merry-go-round, I tried to put it all behind me, and get on with everyday life.

After worrying about this for weeks, and just before I got some of the answers, I felt quite unwell. And sooner rather than later I would be back bender drinking. The benders were getting progressively longer now, and I would often be so ill after a couple of week's non-stop drinking that I would be taken into hospital to dry out, and then back to *AA*.

I couldn't work all of this out on my own. If I could have done it, I would have done by this time – it wasn't for the want of trying. Some days I would be thinking so much that it tired me out, and I had to go and lie down. Sleep would come – it was all too much. Everyday things were different, I could think clear-headedly about my shopping and housework and other mundane tasks.

I was awfully mixed up at this time in my life, but realising now that I had *always* been mixed up. Nobody ever listened to what I was trying to say. Especially when I came out with things like: "Drink's not the problem – someone's *done* this to me!" I had come to the realisation that, whilst alcohol had been causing me social and health problems, this never answered the question '*why*?' Why was I behaving like this? All I ever asked myself for years and years was "what's wrong with me?" – never realising that I was suffering severe periodic depression.

I even resorted to seeking help from my GP. Although frightened to do so, I summoned up the courage to explain that I didn't like *AA*, half expecting him to say that I would just *need* to like it. But instead he suggested that I try the ACA (Ayrshire Council on Alcohol), and telephoned there and then to make an appointment for me to go along the next day.

I came out of the surgery feeling in one way relieved, but equally confused about what they could possibly tell me. After all, when I had visited a fellow-alcoholic in Loudon House, the alcohol treatment annexe of Ailsa psychiatric hospital, I had seen a poster prominently displayed in the entrance hall which proclaimed: *There is no known cure for alcoholism!*

Next day I wearily turned up at the ACA. At that time I thought that they would tell me what was wrong with me, because I thought that's what counselling was, and wondered what it would be. The simple answer is – nothing! As far as I remember, I was just asked how much I was drinking, and told how it might help to alternate fruit juice with my alcoholic drinks, count my weekly intake in 'units', record them in a diary, and try to keep within the recommended limits.

Inwardly I stifled a yawn, and sighed to myself: "I know all this! But I wish you would tell me *why* I am behaving like this! What's wrong with me?"

It was then I decided that nobody else could help me, that never again would I go anywhere else for assistance, that I would just have to help myself, and work out my own cure. After all, my father had always said that if you want a job done well, the best thing is to do it yourself.

I was firmly convinced that there was a cure – regardless of that poster in the hospital – but frightened, too, because if whoever put it up didn't know what it was, or rather didn't believe that there was one, how on earth was I going to discover it?

You may be wondering how I came to think that my problems were coming from my childhood. Well, this is how it came about. A few months later, I had a visit from my brother and his wife. This was the first time we had met up since my mother's funeral, and during the conversation I said quite casually that I was upset and a little bit annoyed about my father's decision to sort out my mother's jewellery when I wasn't there. I dared to say this very gently, because I didn't want to hurt his feelings, and would have been too embarrassed if my words had ever got back to him and he thought that I had been talking about him behind his back.

My brother's wife looked at Gordon, and said to him: "I think she's got a right to know."

"Know what?" I asked.

"It was your *mother* who had said to your father, that if she died first, he was to make sure that you got nothing – especially any of her jewellery – as you had your shop at the time, you would probably just sell it."

"But my mother knew that the shop's been closed for over a year," I replied. I was utterly astonished, and could say no more.

Then my brother asked: "Did you ever do anything to hurt my mother?"

This was adding insult to injury, but was also history repeating itself. My brother couldn't (or wouldn't) believe that his mother could have been at fault; just as I could not see the slightest defect in my father, nor he in his mother. This seems to be a pattern running through many families.

At that, I rushed from the kitchen through to the lounge to stop myself bursting into a flood of tears. After a couple of minutes I managed to compose myself, and rejoin the rest of the family around the kitchen table.

At first there was a silence, and then a chorus of: "Don't take it too seriously – remember that your mother was ill when she said that. Don't let it bother you."

And this is what I tried to do. I felt too upset to do anything else. And when it was time for them to leave, we said our goodbyes, and I sheepishly showed them to the door.

As the evening went on, the subject wasn't mentioned amongst my family – that was supposed to be that. Peace returning to the household was more important. Nobody wanted to be involved or disturbed – it was teatime now, and there were rumblings of 'we're starving!'

I started preparing the evening meal, still reeling from the shocks of the day. But I was trying not to be short-tempered with everyone around me, though I felt like screaming inside. So I took their advice, tried to forget all about it, and after tea decided to have a drink instead. Our home was like a doll's house – we played at *Happy Families*.

But I never did forget about it – at that time I thought about my mother constantly. It was now almost a year after her death, and though I still missed her, I had accepted the fact that she was dead. But I was still upset, and could not understand why my brother thought that I had done something to hurt my mother. I worried this to death for about six months, but none of my family was interested, and I didn't come up with any answers.

Until one night when I was getting ready for bed, I thought that I could detect a faint smell of burning. There was only one thing that it could be, and that was the electric blanket. I pulled back the bedcovers, and saw that the sheets had been scorched. Luckily, nothing had caught alight, and I unplugged the blanket and stripped the bed.

I was quite upset – not because of the scorched sheet, but because the electric blanket had belonged to my mother. It was still new, as she had kept it as a spare, and this was the first time that it had been used.

When I had remade the bed, I suddenly said to myself: "Some of my upset has got something to do with burning! Somebody has done this to me." But further than that, nothing quite made sense yet.

Not until a couple of nights later, when I was coming out of my bath, and caught sight of myself in a full-length mirror, and saw the burn marks on my chest – I suppose really for the first time, as I had always hidden the fact that they were there, even from myself.

I was so shocked, and just stood there, staring at myself in the mirror. Now I was able to recall the whole incident of my being burnt by the poultice, just as it had happened all those years before. It disturbed me for several weeks afterwards, but at least I was beginning to make the right connections, and some things were starting to make sense at last. Of course, I hadn't done anything to hurt my mother – she had hurt me!

When I think about it now, I realise the power of the mind. If you think that your body is strong, the mind is even more powerful. It can go right back into your childhood, and recall things that you thought that you'd forgotten, and travel right around the world, without you even leaving your armchair. All it asks in return is a little rest from time to time!

I had been, and still was, very angry at what my mother had done to me, but feeling unable to express this anger, it was instead turned inwards. And when anger is suppressed rather than expressed, it often emerges as depression, and this had been one of the many causes of my perennial sadness.

I wondered whether this was also one of the reasons why I had once, several years before, deliberately smashed down onto the kitchen worktop a wineglass that I had been washing. The force of the blow drove fragments of glass straight into my hand, severing a tendon on two of my fingers, and requiring six or seven stitches. I now believe that I was trying to cut out the emotional pain that I couldn't figure out then. It gave me something tangible to worry about, something that I could see.

After this, I decided that I would ask all the questions that I wanted to ask, and that I would never stop trying to find out why I had been so upset and sad for most of my adult life.

Things went on much the same for a while after this, seesawing from one upset to another. Then less than two years after my mother's death, my father died.

I was the only one with him in the hospital ward, and it was the first and (so far) only time that I have seen anyone die. It was a harrowing experience, as at the end this strong-willed man was so in need of love and emotional support.

I had never seen this side of him before – he was trying to cling to me for some comfort. With tears running down my face, I couldn't bring myself to respond by putting my arms around him. That sort of demonstration of affection didn't happen in our family – it just wasn't done.

Within ten minutes he was dead, and suddenly in my head I was saying quite loudly to myself over and over again: "I'm free, I'm free!"

Almost as quickly, I clapped a hand to my mouth, shocked at what I was saying. Why was I saying that? Why? I couldn't get the thought out of my head.

I know now that this new-found freedom resulted from the chains that I had allowed to shackle me to my father's rule of law were broken by his death, and I was now responsible for my own decisions. I had nothing to kick back against after he was gone. Soon afterwards I decided to do something about my life, and start making my own rules.

It wasn't long afterwards that Murdoch and I first met, and our getting together was to have a radical effect upon both our lives. We believe now that we were destined to find each other, and had we not done so, this book would not have been written, because probably neither of us would have resolved all our problems alone – we had both tried for long enough.

We got together in the summer of 1993, and planned to get married on Christmas Eve the same year. We both wanted it to be a church wedding, but weren't sure whether this would be possible, as we both had two divorces in our trophy cabinet.

Our parish church was the Auld Kirk of St John the Baptist in Ayr, and we made an appointment to go and see the then minister, the Rev.

T. Alan W. Garrity. We had never met him, but when we did we found him very easy to speak to, and when we told him our problem, he still said that he would be pleased to marry us. For good measure, we also told him about our drink problem, but that didn't seem to put him off either. He just said that he would prefer it if we could possibly turn up at the church for the wedding reasonably sober!

Murdoch, as you will have gathered already, also had a serious alcohol problem. He had enjoyed a public school education – Dulwich College, in London – and had then gone on to Magdalene College, Cambridge. A glittering career should have been assured. By his early thirties he had his own public relations consultancy, and a weekly money programme on radio, which spawned a television series. But for reasons that are another story altogether, he had allowed alcohol to destroy his life, and now his bright future was all behind him. He was out of work, and (apparently) without much prospect of finding any.

Although the long-term effects of our getting together were to prove beneficial for both of us, the initial results were positively catastrophic – and almost fatal.

If you've never suffered from an alcohol problem yourself, you might not be aware that during a bender you can literally 'lose' a week or so in a state of virtual 'black-out'. While this is going on, to other people you will seem perfectly aware of what you are saying and doing, but to all intents and purposes you are not consciously aware of anything. Then suddenly you will come to again, having no idea what day it is, and with only the faintest recollections, if any, of the past days or weeks.

This had often happened to both of us before we met, but now it was happening to us both when we had got together. On one particular occasion, finding out what day it was the last thing on my mind, although it should have been.

I woke up to find myself lying on the lounge floor, with a blanket wrapped round me. Murdoch was on the settee, still deeply asleep, and with his back to me. Slowly and shakily, I managed to get to my feet. I was desperately thirsty, and had to get to the kitchen for a glass of water. There didn't seem to be any booze left, but I probably wouldn't have been able to stomach any even if there had been. I felt as if the alcohol had scorched my insides dry.

My thirst was unquenchable, and was made worse by the fact that I couldn't keep the water down that I drank – for every sip that I managed to take, I would bring up a tumblerful, and my blanket was soon soaking. But now I found that I could no longer walk to the kitchen, but could only crawl to the sink, and pull myself up to the taps after several painful attempts.

An hour or so later, I couldn't even manage this, and tried to waken Murdoch by calling him, but he was still comatose. From where I was lying, I could see the kitchen sink. I could hear the tap running, and the sound of rain lashing the windows. The thought of refreshing cold water was driving me mad. I could just imagine standing outdoors in the torrential downpour, face turned upwards, mouth wide open, and drinking great gulps of it.

I don't know how long this went on, but long enough for me to go from being mad to being sad. I was convinced that I was dying, and just couldn't stop thinking about my children, and that I would never see them or Murdoch again.

Eventually Murdoch stirred and woke up. He too was parched, and brought me a glass of water back from the kitchen. I hadn't got the strength to hold it, so he put it to my lips. But I was still bringing up more bodily fluids than the water I could keep down, and must have been seriously dehydrated. Murdoch realised this, and decided to phone for an ambulance, as I was beginning to slip in and out of consciousness.

I was taken to the Accident & Emergency Department of Ayr Hospital, and all I remember is begging a doctor to give me a glass of water. They were pinching the skin around my stomach to see how long it would take to go back down. After this I was put on a trolley, wheeled into a side room, and put on a saline drip. I caught sight of a clock, and noticed that it was almost four o'clock in the afternoon. And from then until the following morning was one of the scariest and the longest times that I ever remember. I could feel my body beginning to shake and tremble, but I couldn't move – if I had, I would have pulled the drip out. Still convinced that I was going to die, I just had to endure it.

Morning finally arrived and I had survived – the worst was over, but I was still in a hell of a state, and I felt the need for medication, as I still had the shakes, and didn't have the strength to sit up in bed. And it's impossible to contain one's anxiety when coming off alcohol cold turkey.

A bit later on I found out from a nurse what date it was, and to my horror realised it was just three weeks until our wedding day. We had come out of the bender not a moment too soon. Next she told me that Murdoch had also been admitted into hospital, and that he was being moved into the same room with me. And then she said that a Doctor Malek would be coming to see us from Ailsa Hospital, the neighbouring psychiatric unit, and he arrived about lunchtime.

I had expected to be ridiculed, but he had a very calm, pleasant manner, and I felt that he cared. He asked if we would be willing to go into Ailsa for a week or so, and we agreed. There was only one thing – I was so worried how we were going to get there, as neither of us could stand, let alone walk, but he said that he would send an ambulance for us.

This he did, and by mid-afternoon we were admitted into the psychiatric hospital in order to recover. Unfortunately, we were in separate wards, so we could only see each other at certain times. This was unbearable, as we needed to be together, so after three or four days, as soon as we were back on our feet, we signed ourselves out. Dr Malek spoke to each of us on our own before we left.

He told me that I had been even more ill than I thought when I had been brought into hospital, and during that first night the doctors hadn't thought that I had much chance of surviving until the morning, and were quite surprised when I did.

When we got home, we found the house in an utter shambles. Empty bottles, half-empty takeaway cartons and dirty dishes littered the floor in practically every room, and spilt rice had been trodden into the carpets, including up the stairs. We were both still very weak and fragile, but slowly and gradually we started the process of clearing up.

In between bouts of washing-up and sweeping and scrubbing carpets, I also managed, with great difficulty, to have a bath and shampoo my hair. While putting on some make-up, I looked at my face in the mirror, and saw a yellow streak running from the middle of my forehead to my left temple. At first I thought it was just a mark, and tried to wipe it off, but realised that I must be jaundiced, as the whites of my eyes had a definite yellowish tinge as well. I was really scared.

It was a rotten few days, but a couple of nice things did happen. First, Alan Garrity called round to see us. While we were in hospital we had had to phone and cancel an appointment that we had to see him to make final arrangements for the wedding, and he had come to see if we were all right. We had to tell him what had happened. He was puzzled by alcoholism, but had asked some of his fellow-ministers about it, and they had told him that *AA* seemed to be the best solution available.

I had told him a bit about my childhood, and that I didn't agree with the chemical dependency theory. It didn't feel right, surely it's *why* you are behaving in the way you are that's the question we should really be asking. He thought about it for a moment, and then said he agreed.

"One of the things that I've noticed," I went on, "is that you rarely if ever see an alcoholic who's been blind from birth. I think that this is because they have been nurtured and given special attention, in order that they can achieve as much independence as possible."

"If all children, not just ones with a serious disability, were treated with the same care, attention and respect, alcoholism and other related so-called illnesses or diseases would not be as prevalent as they are. If my family had done so with me, life might have bent me, but it would never have broken me."

The next morning a beautiful bunch of flowers was delivered to the door, accompanied by a get-well-soon card from the church. That cheered us up a bit.

We knew that Alan meant well, but we weren't convinced by what he had said about *AA* being the best solution. Nevertheless, we decided that we would have to stay off drinking for the time being and go back to *AA*, although deep in my heart I knew that this was not the final solution. But my benders were getting progressively worse over the years, because the longer I went on failing to work the whole thing out, the more depressed I became, and the more I wanted to drink, desperate to be free.

As we started going to meetings again, our fair-weather friends came back. So much so that two long-standing married members, Tom and Nancy, who were each then at least 25 years sober, volunteered to be best man and matron of honour at our wedding. Not a single member of either my family or Murdoch's chose to attend the ceremony, so we were glad that half-a-dozen *AA* members came along, and then back to the house for some Christmas fayre that I had prepared, with fruit juice, tea or coffee to go with it. It was not the wedding day that I would have chosen, but at that time it was the one that had to be. Murdoch and I were just happy to be together and married.

A week or so later, I bumped into another couple of long-standing *AA* members, Betty and Bob, who knew we were back at meetings. They apologised for not having been able to come to the wedding, but said that they would like to come and visit us sometime. I told them that Tom and Nancy were coming that afternoon for tea, so why didn't they join us?

Although we didn't agree with their ideas, we were trying our best to fit in, and decided to try and keep the conversation off anything to do with alcoholism. For the first week or so coming off a bender, I am so overwhelmed and easily intimidated, but now more than a month had gone by, and I knew that I would give as good as I got.

But it's impossible to keep *AA* members off their favourite subject.

They were hardly in the house two minutes when Bob started up: "I hope you're going to do your ninety meetings in ninety days!"

I thought to myself: "Here we go again!" – but simply answered: "No, it's a normal life that I'm wanting to live, not an artificial one."

Betty and Nancy chipped in: "With your past record, you seem to need it drummed into you. Remember you're dealing with alcohol – cunning, baffling and powerful!"

"I don't agree with that," I said. "Powerful, yes. Lots of drugs are. But not cunning or baffling. If you think of bottles of alcohol displayed in any shop window, they are inanimate objects. It's what's going on in your mind when you drink alcohol – that's the problem. If it's all right in other people, you need to sort out what's going on in your own mind."

She just looked at me. She said: "You're very, very sick. I've been sober for twenty-five years – I'm wise."

"If you were wise, Nancy, you'd be able to drink like any normal person. I don't think that so-called alcoholism has got anything to do with drink. I always knew that there was something that I was unhappy about in my life, even as far back as my childhood, long before I ever touched alcohol.

"I'm desperately trying to put my life back together. Although I haven't worked it all out yet, I know that if I do, I'll be able to drink normally again."

"Normally again! That's the great obsession of every abnormal drinker – it says so in the *Big Book*," argued Nancy.

"So what's wrong with that? It's natural to want to find out what's wrong, put it right, and then have the same privileges as everyone else, including the freedom and ability to drink normally again. Nobody wants to be an alcoholic. But anybody else would feel the same as me who'd enjoyed a drink, and then were diagnosed as an alcoholic. It's my right to be the same as everybody else. They have choices, and I want the freedom to have choices too. Is there something wrong with that?

"I respect what you've done, but I think that you and *AA* members like you have won a battle, but lost the war!"

At that Nancy just looked at me in dumbstruck silence, unable to find an answer to what I had said. She sighed, then signalled to Tommy, who was just sitting quietly, that she wanted to leave, and Betty and Bob went with them, shaking their heads at me, equally bewildered. "You don't seem to be able to understand that it's the first drink that sets up the compulsion," was Bob's parting shot. So that was the end of what could have been a pleasant afternoon.

The next few weeks were not a particularly good time for us. On the one hand, we were frightened of having to endure another bender. On the other we knew that, for us, going to *AA* meetings was never going to last. And to cap it all, Murdoch wasn't working.

Out of the blue one day we hit on the idea of making a fresh start by moving away from Ayr to Cambridge. Although we knew at the back of our minds that we would merely be taking our problems with us, we thought that, if Murdoch could go back to Magdalene College and study for his PhD, maybe, just maybe, things would be different, and we could make a new beginning.

We contacted the College and requested all the necessary application forms and other paperwork, but that was all that we did in the way of plans and preparations. I had never been to Cambridge before, and most other people would first have made an exploratory trip to a town they were planning to move to, in order to arrange some accommodation, if nothing else, but not us!

A week later, we loaded all our worldly goods, my best furniture, and Murdoch's trusty word processor, into a van we had hired, and set off with little more than a wing and a prayer, and Caruso my pet canary in his cage to keep us company, and drove off into the twilight.

That journey was a nightmare. We left at about ten o'clock at night, and were expecting (at the latest) to arrive in Cambridge soon after breakfast the following morning. But the van, weighed down by all our accoutrements, struggled gamely on, puffing and panting all the way, but could only on rare occasions manage 40 mph, when a rare burst of energy and a fortunate fair following wind came upon it. On one occasion, I remember that we were rather ignominiously passed in the fast lane by a farmer on his tractor and trailer, spraying foul-smelling manure in his wake!

Dawn found us only a few miles down the M6 motorway, grabbing a coffee and a bite to eat for Murdoch at a service station. Soon after, the sun began to shine with a vengeance and, fearing that Caruso might shortly expire in the heat, I gave him a fine spray from time to time with some fresh cold water just to cool him down.

We eventually struggled into Cambridge at about 5 o'clock in the evening, which didn't allow us much time to find somewhere to stay. So we decided to book into a bed and breakfast for the night, and start our search for more long-term accommodation first thing the following morning.

The early edition of the *Cambridge Evening News* hits the streets about 10 am, and we purchased one of the first copies from John, the news vendor in Bridge Street. We chatted to him then, and got to know him quite well during our stay in Cambridge.

When we left him, we started to trawl through the 'Rooms to Let' advertisements. But nobody seemed willing to take us in with all my furniture. Time passed, and evening was approaching again…

Fortunately, the last number we called seemed more hopeful. We took the details, including the address, and said we would drive round straight away.

The woman who answered the door didn't seem particularly pleasant, but by that time we could no longer afford to be too fussy. She had bare feet, and her house had bare floorboards. It was also scantily furnished, so she didn't seem too upset at the prospect of temporarily housing mine. Her eyes lit up the evening gloom when we said that we could give her a deposit and one month's rent in advance, and when she realised that we could pay it in cash, they became positively fluorescent.

We were in! Apart from the mere formality of carrying sideboards and fridges etc. up the garden path into the house, but fortunately our new landlady had a tame and well-trained lodger *in situ*, who was now rapidly dragooned into service, and patiently broke his back ferrying my heaviest belongings into our new home.

Murdoch and I were not idle either, rummaging away in the recesses of that dusty van, but even after all our exertions, we found that the bathroom was even dirtier than we were, but beggars can't be choosers. Amazingly, sweet dreams followed.

There was one more difficulty about our new accommodation that we didn't discover until the following morning – our new landlady's cat! Caruso was obviously not safe in this establishment, but fortunately there was an old folks' home right next door, and they were only too delighted to take him under their wing. Although judging by the way my feathered friend took to his new companions, perhaps I should say that he took the old folk under *his* wing!

We were so thrilled to have arrived safely in Cambridge, and for the first few weeks it was just like a holiday, looking round all the Colleges and places of interest. We even managed to visit Murdoch's old tutor Arthur Sale, who was delighted to see us and gave us a lovely welcome. He claimed to serve the best coffee in East Anglia - it was accompanied by fine slithers of dark Bournville chocolate and rich wholemeal biscuits, of which Murdoch took one, but not me.

But once Murdoch had shown me all the sights of Cambridge, the party was over. We needed to get back to some kind of normality, but this was not easy. Looking round, we realised that what we had created for ourselves was just another nightmare.

There we were, stuck in this small double room, which was filled with boxes. There were boxes almost jamming the door on the way in, there were boxes on top of the bed and under the bed. There was no wardrobe – only a rail which spanned a small recess in one wall, and on which there was scarcely room for my clothes – most of them had to be left in suitcases. And the suitcases had boxes on top of them, so you can imagine the frustration of trying to find clean clothes every day!

We had our portable television balanced precariously on top of a small bedside cabinet, and to add to our discomfort, our landlady didn't seem to care whether things in her house worked or not. The curtains in our bedroom hung with one hook at each end and one in the middle, and they would neither close nor open. She always left her dirty dishes clogging the sink all day. So did the other lodger, but at least when he got home from his work, he always apologised and tried to make up for it by doing some of her chores.

There seemed no way out of this situation – we couldn't afford a flat of our own. We had quite literally boxed ourselves into a corner!

We had told our landlady the day we moved in that we were alcoholics, and that she should never offer us a drink. By now it was at least a couple of months since our last drink, and I was really imagining a refreshing gin and tonic with plenty of ice and a slice of lemon or lime in my best crystal glasses. And do you know what? Before you could say 'peas', Murdoch was down at the corner shop, and concealing his purchases underneath his coat on his way back into the house. Suddenly, I began to feel a bit more human again! But this was to be the beginning of our downfall...

We stayed upstairs drinking for the best part of three days, which must have unnerved our landlady. Because some time whilst we were sleeping she removed our door keys, and when we next woke up, demanded that we leave immediately. She kept most of the money we had paid her as a deposit, and said that we should phone her when we had sobered up and could make arrangements to collect our possessions.

I have already told you in Chapter 1 what happened on this bender over the next couple of weeks, and how we woke up at the end on Christ's Pieces, were befriended by two nurses in Market Square, and ended up at in the homeless hostel at 222 Victoria Road. We left the story with Murdoch and I selling newspapers at McDonald's Corner...

Chapter Five
The Final Furlong

Now does my project gather to a head.

William Shakespeare: **The Tempest**

OUR job selling newspapers was not to last much longer. Winter was fast approaching, and we were getting tired of the long, dark, cold wet days that left us drenched to the skin, and our fingers almost frost-bitten. Although I wasn't standing as long at a time as Murdoch, it was getting more and more difficult because of the peripheral neuritis. I had a tingling sensation in my legs, and my feet had an aching numbness, which was relieved by wearing an elasticated bandage and two pairs of Murdoch's socks. But this made it very difficult to get my boots on!

I was also very embarrassed at being seen out in my sewn-up coat, which was the only waterproof one I had. And things were made even worse when I took a haemorrhage in my eye, which was happening quite regularly every two or three weeks, probably because of the stress and strain of our situation. Every day I would wear my chunky heavily laden silver charm bracelet and expensive engagement ring to divert people's attention from my bedraggled look, trying to let them know that I had seen better times than this – I was so ashamed of myself. But I didn't want anybody's sympathy, because underneath I knew that I was just as good as the next person.

Enough was soon enough, and we handed in our notice. The advantage of this was that it gave us time to trawl through the recruitment advertisements in the newspapers, looking for anything at all that might be suitable, and that preferably wouldn't entail standing out in the street all day.

We hadn't decided whether to stay in Cambridge and pursue the PhD idea, or to go back to Ayr, so we decided to cover every eventuality. Murdoch visited the Director of Studies in English Literature at his old college to discuss what would be involved in doing research. That would have been my choice. But as well as this, every day we would walk down to the main Cambridge public library, complete with note-pads and pens, and trawl through all the recruitment advertisements in all the English national daily newspapers. And then we got my daughter Elaine to send us the *Ayrshire Post* every week as well.

Having listed every possibility, Murdoch would type out application letters on the word processor, attach copies of his newly reconstructed CV, and off we would trudge in the late afternoon to put them in the post. The cost of the stamps, the photocopying, not to mention the paper and envelopes, took up a significant portion of our weekly budget, so it meant that we didn't have a lot left over, even for basic necessities.

Nothing much came of all our hard work. We must have sent out at least 80–100 applications, but most of the time we didn't even get a reply. As December wore on, our initial burst of energy and enthusiasm began to wane, and with Christmas only a couple of days away, we decided to take a break until after the festive season was over, and hope that things would begin to improve again then.

Money was very tight – in fact, every penny was a prisoner. One day a small disaster happened while we were doing our shopping. Murdoch was holding on tightly to a handful of loose change, when someone bumped into him in the street. A couple of pound coins slipped from his grasp, and rolled down a nearby drain as we watched helplessly. I burst out crying, the disappointment was too much.

About that time, we moved from our small single rooms in the main block, over to two adjoining bedsits in the block where we had spent our first weekend. It wasn't great, but a distinct improvement. One room, which we used as our bedroom and sitting room, I had succeeded in making quite cosy. The other was where we kept the word-processor, and anything else of value that we didn't want to risk keeping in the lock-up garage in case it was broken into.

It was much quieter than in the main building. There were four rooms on each corridor, each sharing one kitchen and a bathroom, which we all kept spotless.

We still had to use the main building – apart from anything else, it was the only way in and out of the hostel – and also we had to go over to the office everyday to collect our mail. New people were coming in all the time, and others were leaving, but over the months we did begin to get to know some of the residents.

One person I remember was Paul Knight, who came from Milton Keynes, and with whom we used to have long chats. He was desperately trying to sort himself out. But he moved on soon afterwards, and we never heard from him again.

Then there was Jackie, who was a heroin addict. She was getting medical attention for her legs, which were covered with holes caused by old abscesses. She had arrived from London, to join her partner John, who already had a room in the hostel. Jackie was in such a bad way that I offered her a pair of sandals and some of Murdoch's socks to wear, as she had been wandering around barefoot.

John, who was an expert shoplifter, must have appreciated this, and asked us if there was anything we wanted for Christmas that he could purloin for us on his next expedition. "Perfume, cigarettes, drinks, chocolates, something new to wear – you name it, I'll get it for you!" We politely declined, but one day we met him as he was just setting off on one of his expeditions, dressed in a huge overcoat, with voluminous 'poacher's pockets'.

Unfortunately, his trip could not have been very successful, as we heard later that he had been arrested. Jackie left the hostel soon afterwards, and we never saw either of them again.

The next day – Christmas Eve – was our first wedding anniversary, and I was feeling a bit low in spirits. We would both have loved to have gone out for a good meal and a bottle of wine, or whatever else we fancied to drink. But for the time being we put this thought out of our heads, and compromised instead by going for a coffee at *The Eagle* – an old coaching inn situated in Ben'et Street. We would both have preferred to have gone for a drink. But if we had done so, we would probably have wanted to take a bottle back with us, and alcohol was strictly forbidden in the hostel.

Inside *The Eagle* the atmosphere was cosy and convivial, and the three bars on different levels were all full of people celebrating. But we felt out of it.

Firstly because we must have been the only ones drinking coffee – nothing wrong with coffee, if that's what you fancy, but it's hardly a Christmas drink.

And the second reason we felt excluded was that, although it would have been easy to have allowed ourselves to be drawn into conversation – everybody seemed to be chatting freely to everybody else – we were afraid that someone might recognise us from when we had been selling newspapers, or find out that Murdoch had been to the University and ask him what he had been doing since, or (worst of all) inquire where we were staying now!

So we finished our coffees, and headed back to Victoria Road. In order to give ourselves a breath of fresh air, we turned off Bridge Street into Portugal Place to take the route across Jesus Green.

The afternoon was already getting dark, and on our way we came to a large house with lights blazing from the ground floor front windows.

There didn't seem to be anyone in the room at the time, and for some reason we both stopped to look in.

There was a log fire burning in the grate, and on one side of it there was a huge Christmas tree festooned with glowing decorations, and all around it lay presents wrapped and tied with ribbon. The entire centre of the room was taken up by a large polished mahogany table laid for dinner. And some dinner it was going to be! There were places set for twelve people, with the silver gleaming and the crystal glasses and decanters at each end of the table sparkling in the reflected light, red candles waiting in their holders to be lit, and a centrepiece of beautifully arranged flowers.

Neither of us said a word as we turned away into the gathering dusk, with only the prospect of Christmas Day in the workhouse to look forward to...

We have been asked on more than one occasion recently why we always thought it so important to be able to drink again.

Our answer to that is – it's *not* important for everybody. Some people are quite happy to abstain, and there's nothing wrong with that.

But for us, believing as we did that alcohol was not the real problem (*we* were) being able to drink in a socially acceptable fashion again would prove to ourselves that we had really overcome our psychological problems.

And, in addition, alcohol is a natural part of our culture, especially on special occasions – birthdays, weddings, funerals, as well as Christmas – and not being able to partake fully in these festivities emphasised the sense of social exclusion which was already helping to fuel my depression.

Meanwhile, back in that winter of 1994, we just had to make the best of a bad situation. The next day I cooked a chicken for us, and we had a makeshift Christmas dinner on our own. At least I could eat adequately now, even without having a drink first, although it was still strictly portion-controlled. Apart from that, the so-called festive period passed off uneventfully, and we were soon back on the treadmill of sending off daily job applications.

Several weeks passed without any sign of success, and I began to think that things were never going to get any better. Especially when Murdoch decided that it was not the right thing to do to try for his PhD. It didn't make sense, he said, three or four years of going back to being a student, and no more likely to get a job at the end of it all. Now I was sure that things were never going to get any better.

Later that day, a grey February afternoon, we were doing our shopping at Sainsbury's in Sidney Street. I was looking for some lemonade, but happened to catch sight of the wines and spirits aisle instead. The idea suddenly occurred to me that a bottle of gin would go down very nicely that evening, so I popped one in the trolley. Murdoch was outraged when he saw what I had done, but gave in gradually as he realised that I was quite determined. I assured him that I had got myself and my life sorted out, and that we could now drink quite safely.

And as it turned out, he enjoyed it just as much as I did. I cooked us a nice meal, and we got out my crystal decanter and glasses in honour of the gin, which we had managed to smuggle into the hostel hidden under Murdoch's overcoat. It was a very pleasant evening, which lasted into the early hours of the morning.

After a brief nap we both awoke about 5.30 am, and we didn't need to say anything – we both knew that we wanted to carry on drinking. There was a drop left in the bottle, which gave us enough energy to get up, get dressed and slip out of the hostel. We managed this unnoticed, because there must have been a storm in the night, and part of the side fencing was blown down, allowing us a way out without using the main door.

We were down at the nearest licensed grocer a few minutes before it opened at 6 o'clock, and luckily it wasn't late in opening. We bought a half bottle to see us through till later, when we could buy a bottle cheaper at Sainsbury's, and made our way furtively back the way we had come.

We were back on a bender. Completely different to the last one, when we had been out in the cold most nights, unable to find anywhere to stay. This time we had accommodation, but where we had to be constantly on our guard, as we could have been thrown out if any of the staff had caught us with a drink.

Leo, who stayed in the bedsit next to us along the corridor, reluctantly helped us by offering to discreetly dispose of our empty bottles for us, and by distracting the attention of any of the night shift coming round on their tours of inspection.

And so the bender went on, and might have continued longer, but it was to come to an abrupt and unexpected ending. One day we had been ravenously hungry while we had been out shopping for drink, and had brought half a dozen sausage rolls back with us as well. We had put these in the oven, but then unfortunately had fallen asleep.

The next thing we knew we were surrounded by thick clouds of black smoke, and two hefty firemen were shaking us awake. As soon as it had been established that there was no fire, Neville, the hostel manager and Julia came in, saw our half-empty bottle and glasses, and we were well and truly nicked!

Actually, they were more than understanding. They arranged for us to see Christine Hugh-Jones, a sympathetic doctor who held a weekly surgery at the hostel, and did a lot of work for the homeless.

Dr Hugh-Jones warned us that neither of us could carry on drinking like that for much longer. It was getting too severe, and that one of these times, one or both of us was not going to survive a bender. I didn't need to be told this. You'll remember that, coming off the bender we had a month or so before we had left Ayr, Doctor Malek had said much the same thing.

She prescribed a week's course of librium tablets for each of us, to help with the alcohol withdrawal symptoms, plus some vitamin pills. Like naughty children, hostel inmates were not trusted with their own medication, but had to report to the office three times a day to receive their dose.

Although Neville and Julia had to issue us with a written four weeks' notice to quit our accommodation, they also said that, if we didn't drink during that time, we would be allowed to stay on.

It wasn't long before we got back on our feet, and we just had to start again where we had left off. But I was absolutely devastated by what had happened.

I had been 100% sure that if you got to the root cause of your problems, that would be enough – things would sort themselves out, and you would be able to drink normally again.

By delving back into my past, I had come to understand that my drinking had arisen partly as an escape from my regime of strict dieting – when I drank, I also allowed myself to eat. And, at the same time, as a 'kick back' against the authoritarian upbringing given to me by my parents and my grandmother – a kick back that was all the more effective because of my father's and my grandmother's strictly teetotal background.

I understood so clearly where it all came from, so why had I not been able to stop bendering? This was the thorny question I could not answer, and it left me bewildered, especially in my fragile state after our most recent drinking bout.

Fear of having another bender was raging inside me, especially as each one was further damaging my relationship with my daughter, so I persuaded Murdoch that we should go back to *AA* again. I felt that we were so isolated – we had only made friends with one or two people at the hostel, and they had moved on, and most doors were closed to us back in Ayr. Sometimes I asked myself whether I really existed, but

Murdoch was always there to reassure me. At least *AA* meetings would be company for us both.

During the first meeting we went back to, I told one or two people that we had had a drink, and a member called John overheard the conversation. He jumped up out of his chair, roaring and shouting and pointing his finger, ridiculing 'idiots' like us who couldn't grasp the *AA* programme. "I've no sympathy with you, you bring it on yourself," he said.

"I don't want your sympathy," I replied, "it's some understanding that I'm looking for."

"You'll get all the understanding that you need in the *Big Book*!" he shouted, still pointing his finger.

"But I don't agree with lots of things in the *Big Book*," I pointed out, "and I'd like to be able to discuss it."

I had said the unforgivable in *AA* – especially to the long-time members – only fools dared to disagree with the *Big Book*. John was advancing towards me, seething, and practically foaming at the mouth, and a couple of other members actually had to restrain him. "Don't let her upset you, John," one of them said to him. "She'll learn."

I've often heard it said in *AA* that anger is a luxury that a recovering alcoholic cannot afford. But in fact I've seen many exhibitions of out-of control rage by *AA* members which they often excuse by calling them "dry drunks" – meaning that their behaviour is sometimes worse than when they were drinking. To me, the truth is that these childish tantrums are just a symptom or a sign that whatever is the underlying problem has never been addressed or sorted out.

After the meeting, everybody was standing in groups chatting, but not to us. When I said anything to anyone, they just answered briefly, then turned their back on me. Although this was the worst instance that happened to me personally, during the many years I had been in and out of the fellowship, and in several different parts of the country, I had witnessed many times this sort of tactic – often adopted towards new members and people coming back to *AA* after a 'slip', because that is when we are at our most fragile and vulnerable. It's what they call 'tough love', and try to excuse it by saying that "it's for your own good".

One common example of their bullyboy attitude is when they order: "Take the cotton wool out of your ears, and stuff it in your mouth!" The offending member or new recruit is then told to sit at the front of the room, and "learn to listen, and listen to learn!"

On the way back to the hostel, Murdoch said to me: "What on earth would we want to go back there for? Why don't we just try to do it on our own, without those ignoramuses?"

"But it's not everybody at *AA* that acts like that," I replied. "I've met some lovely people there. Let's give it to the end of the week, and hope that we meet some more sensible people at another meeting."

Murdoch agreed, and the next night we went to a *Big Book* discussion meeting. I hadn't been to one before, and thought that it would be good, because I assumed that at a discussion meeting people actually would be able to discuss the *Big Book*, and I might get some of the insight that I was so desperately seeking.

Silly me! There was actually no discussion about the *Big Book* at all. Instead, a well-thumbed copy of it was passed round the meeting, and everybody took a turn at reading a few pages. Except for Murdoch and I – the last time we had done anything like that was in the infants' school, and we weren't anxious to repeat the experience.

About half-way through the meeting I dared to ask what the point of it all was – the writers of the *Big Book* themselves say that it is only a *suggested* programme (they said they couldn't answer the riddle) yet here it was being treated as if it was the Ten Commandments, and set in stone for eternity.

Hardly had I got the words out of my mouth, when a woman called Penelope, a rather lean, resplendent figure, flung her arms in the air, and started gesticulating wildly. "My goodness!" she said, "We can't have this! Please let's get on with the meeting!"

And so they did, purposefully and studiously choosing to ignore my interruption. And after the meeting, we got the same cold shoulder treatment that we had received the previous evening. Except that, coming down the stairs, someone said to me: "You should read 'The Doctor's Opinion' in the *Big Book*!"

"I have," I replied, "and that's what I would have liked to talk about during the meeting."

Then someone else said: "I've been coming to *AA* meetings at least three nights a week for sixteen years. Drink's not important."

I looked at him and replied: "What do you mean – it *must* be important if you've been talking about it for sixteen years!"

He just looked at me in silence.

There were meetings every night somewhere in Cambridge, but we gave *AA* a miss for a few evenings, since after the last two meetings I was feeling worse than before I had went. But then we decided to go back to the Sunday night church hall meeting in Emmanuel Street – the first meeting we had been to in Cambridge. It had been a cold bleak day in early March, and we felt in need of some spiritual nourishment – that first candlelit meeting had been so nice.

But this time, apart from the familiar face of Frank, there were only half-a-dozen people there, and nobody was speaking – just shuffling their feet and clearing their throats nervously.

I thought that I would start off by saying what had happened to me at the two previous meetings, daring to suggest that I didn't agree with

the *Big Book*. I suggested that our problems originated in our childhood, and asked if anybody agreed.

But my question was just ignored, so afterwards, rather than face
the same cold shoulder treatment again, we made our excuses, and left
earlier than usual, calling out goodnight to everyone as we made our
exit.

One day in early Spring, Murdoch and I had gone to do some shopping in Market Square. We had just finished putting some fruit that we
had bought into a bag, when we caught sight of Frank coming towards
us. There wasn't that much space between the lines of market stalls,
and he could hardly failed to have seen us. But he bent his head away
from us, and hurried on past, avoiding looking in our direction. That's
the sort of treatment that you come to expect from many long-time
members of *AA* when you fail to conform. It had happened to us so
often before in Ayr.

I agreed with Murdoch by this time that, for us, any more *AA* meetings were quite out of the question. They never gave you a chance to
suggest different ideas – it was their way or nothing. And their way was
totally opposite to the one I still wanted to pursue. *AA* says that 'the
only requirement for membership is a desire to stop drinking' – but I
didn't want to stop drinking, just to stop drinking *alcoholically*. And I
believe that most alcoholics feel the same. As it says in Chapter 3 in the
Big Book: "The idea that somehow, some day he will control and enjoy
his drinking is the great obsession of every abnormal drinker."

No wonder they're obsessed. Who wouldn't be? Nobody likes being
denied one of life's simple pleasures, or being socially excluded. So
how do you respond when you are? You pretend the opposite, especially to the world outside, smile, and say how marvellous *AA* is. But
the more they pretend, the more they bang the big drum in praise of
AA, the more they box themselves in until it becomes difficult to do an
about-turn and admit the truth.

In spite of everything that had happened, I still believed that it was possible for Murdoch and I to be able to drink responsibly again.

I was sure that I was on the right path, but obviously there was more to work out before I found the final solution.

I had to go back over everything that had gone wrong in my life. As I did so, I came to realise that, as well as sorting out and understanding the past, it was also necessary to rectify the inlaid patterns of my negative thinking in the present. This negative thinking was caused by the past. My family had continued to treat me as a child, and I was still thinking as I did as a child, even when I grew older and left home. For me, growing up had not been allowed. And, being unaware of this, I carried on with my inappropriate behaviour, acting in an immature, childish fashion in key crucial situations in my adult life.

Instead of responding in a mature and positive manner, firstly by accepting that I had created the situation, and secondly realising that I had done my best and could do no more, I had reacted to disappointments by thinking that everything was hopeless. Which led me to think that *I* was useless, that nothing would ever change, and that I just needed an escape. And my escape was booze. I didn't have then the solid sense of myself necessary to see that I and my health were more important than any situation.

So, just as over the years I had gradually changed the superficial aspects of my inherited behaviour, like my obsessive cleaning, now I also resolved to tackle the fundamentals, and cultivate a more mature response to life's adversities.

And in fact during the next six months we had an occasional evening drinking, (when we could afford it – we were also trying to save money), and there were no unfortunate consequences whatsoever. Although I couldn't be sure that benders were finally over – and in fact they weren't yet quite – nevertheless, as my awareness increased stage by stage, so gradually did my drinking problem improve, and the benders became more infrequent.

It took six months before anything turned up for us on the work front. It was a long, hot, difficult summer for us to get through, not knowing where we were going, or what was going to happen to us. But for the first time I was beginning to cope better with everything, and we flung ourselves back into the daily routine of job applications with renewed enthusiasm.

And at last our persistence paid off. Eventually a market research company wrote to say that they had work coming up in Ayrshire in the near future, and we replied straight away accepting their offer. This, coupled with the chance of a computer course for Murdoch in Ayr itself, was enough to decide us upon heading back to Scotland. So we started planning accordingly, and my daughter Elaine, who had recently heard me talking in a more positive way during my weekly telephone calls, seemed a bit happier about our coming home, and she agreed to make all the necessary arrangements at her end.

It was a great relief to get back into a normal house again. After a year of walking on cement floors covered with rough industrial carpeting, we were once again back to the comfort of Axminster (at least it felt like Axminster to us), and the privacy of our own kitchen and bathroom, which we had previously had to share. The joy of our own front door – and the freedom of walking in and out at will without the possibility of being searched, and of having people coming to call on us without their having to be issued with a pass. And our own telephone ringing for us once again! We couldn't resist the temptation of a few glasses of gin to celebrate, and happily there was no suggestion of a bender the next day.

But the novelty soon began to wear off. The house that had seemed so luxurious when we first got back soon began to reveal an alarmingly long list of defects needing repair – a cracked wash-hand basin, a cooker with only two gas rings working, and a leaking washing machine just for starters!

What made matters even worse was the fact that, after the computer course, the only job that the market research company came up with entailed Murdoch walking from one end of Paisley to the other in rain, hail or snow, ringing the doorbells of people who were mostly out at work. Without a car, it was horrendous, and made selling newspapers in Cambridge seem a comparative doddle in retrospect.

On top of it all, we were almost as isolated as we had been in Cambridge. Although Elaine lived close by, she was still wary, and kept a safe distance. Apart from her, we had no real friends – they had all gone, and no social life whatsoever. The only people we knew in Ayr were *AA* members, and with their arrogant assumption that theirs is the only way to deal with a drink problem, most drop you like a hot potato if you don't 'follow their path'.

There was one final bender, but nothing as dramatic as the ones we had undergone previously.

As soon as we did finally manage to get off that bender, we decided to give *AA* one last chance, as fear coming off a bender over-rules reason, and leaves you totally shattered. However, to us it was just as insufferable as ever, and made no more sense than it did before. And I soon noticed the superficial happiness masking the sadness of a lot of the members, for I had been the same.

So one evening we came home from a meeting and sat down to talk things over. We had been off the drink for quite a while, and our post-bender nerves had gained the time to settle themselves a bit. Moreover, the fear that had taken us back to *AA* was no longer strong enough to hold us there, and the thought of going to meetings for the rest of our lives was just totally unacceptable. It is such an artificial life.

What still had to change even more so was how I was reacting in the here and now to life's disappointments and difficulties. If that didn't change, the benders would probably never stop altogether. But now that at last I saw the full picture, understood my childhood *and* had changed my behaviour, it only remained for me to take the time to let it all sink in, that was crucial. I had been going too quickly, but eventually everything just snapped into place – I had taken another step forward. 'What wound did ever heal but by degrees?'

But everything was such a mess. We had to replace our old word processor and television, which had both been damaged on the journey home, and we had also incurred various other debts before we went to Cambridge. I was so worried about how we were going to manage, that I had taken another haemorrhage in my eye, and my arms were covered in a nervous rash.

The only income we had was from market research, which Murdoch was willing to go on doing, despite the frequent soakings he was getting in the miserable weather. But one night he came home absolutely drenched to the skin, and the sandwiches I had made him were a soggy and inedible mush.

I almost burst into tears, but instead grabbed hold of the company's laptop computer in its waterproof case, and slung it out of the front door for his erstwhile employers to come and collect, to be quickly followed by sealed black bin bags containing the mountains of paperwork that his job also entailed. He handed in his notice the next day.

We didn't relish the thought of going back onto Social Security benefit, but anything was better than market research. However, there was a problem. Because Murdoch had resigned voluntarily, and not been dismissed, it wasn't even certain that we would get any benefit straight away.

So we went round to the Jobcentre, and explained how the work was impossible to do without a car. Also, that he would often find himself needing the toilet, miles from the nearest public convenience, and having to knock on the door of a suspicious householder, and ask if he could use their bathroom.

The woman at the Jobcentre took down all the details, but then asked Murdoch for proof of the size of the area he had been required to cover

in his job. Fortunately, for his last assignment, he had bought himself
a street map of Paisley, and before he went out each day had carefully
marked the location of all the houses that he had to visit.

This he produced, and it provided ample evidence of the problems he
had come up against. Most of the red crosses were nowhere near the
town centre, but far away on the outskirts. Even I was amazed at the
distances that he had needed to walk. How he had managed to keep it
up for so long without a single complaint, I don't know.

But at least we encountered no further problem with our benefit
claim – the first payment arrived the very next week.

So although we didn't have much money coming in, at least we knew
that we could survive. And to give us a small financial cushion we sold
the Pentax camera that Murdoch had bought himself shortly before
we met. This really upset me, because he is a good photographer, and
I knew that he really loved his camera. But he insisted that we sell it,
and we managed to get £100 for it at a local shop, which meant that we
were solvent again and could afford a few little extras, like getting a
haircut and a pair of shoes mended.

Less than six months later, we both got a job-share with a national
charity. Weekday evenings, and during the day at weekends Murdoch
would telephone people trying to persuade them to raise funds by
selling raffle tickets. I handled all the administration and paperwork –
which could be quite onerous, especially as each successive raffle drew
to a close, and all the money would start pouring in. But we kept at it
– at least we could do it at home, and not out in the cold. We quickly
built up the trust of Ann, our supervisor, and it wasn't long before she
was asking us to take on her duties whenever she went on holiday.

So gradually things started getting better. We would work all week,
including during the day on Saturdays and Sundays, but come Saturday night we would open a bottle of wine. Although we both wanted
to drink, and enjoyed these pleasant and relaxing evenings, the fear of
a bender was still there. So much so, in fact, that I would waken on

Sunday mornings trembling at the thought of one happening, as drinking itself was one of the triggers that reminded me of very bad times in my life.

But after breakfast and a few coffees and realising that neither of us felt like a drink, and we could get on with the rest of our day.

And it was just the same with my eating. I wasn't exactly dieting – in fact at the weekend when we had a drink, we would also have a damned good feed! But during the week, it was back to counting calories – I was eating well and healthily enough, but I still lacked the confidence to be the real me. And without the real me coming out, I wasn't truly happy. I didn't feel able to take the last few steps, and eat and drink whenever and how much I wanted. It was just the balance that was lacking, and also the self-belief that I could achieve it. The last mile home's the longest, and took me at least a year to make it.

It was very difficult. Without perhaps fully realising it, we were both still 'controlling' our drinking; or rather our drinking was still controlling us. We would watch our intake, and we would certainly not drink during the week. And I had the additional problem of controlling (or being controlled by) my eating.

The fact that things weren't yet quite right was brought home to me one time when Elaine invited me to her flat for a midweek hen-night with a couple of her friends after I'd finished work. By this time she had realised how well we were doing compared to the past, and had come to trust us a bit more. She was on holiday from her work, and she was planning a nice supper and what had now become one of our favourites – some red wine.

The prospect of this scared me somewhat. I could imagine there being all the delicious but fattening nibbles before supper, which I loved, and then something like pizza and French fries on top of that. As if that wasn't bad enough, there was also the problem of the "blushful Hippocrene". I was fearful of having a drink during the week – what if it led to a bender?

Eventually I did decide to go. I nursed a single glass of wine all evening, barely ate anything at all, and the tension I was feeling rather spoilt the enjoyment of the evening for me.

I was talking to Elaine about this a few days later, and she said something to me that was quite illuminating: "Mum, I appreciate how much better you are now, and I certainly wouldn't like you to go back to drinking and going on benders the way you used to. But you don't need to keep such an iron grip either – you should be more spontaneous, and eat and drink when you feel like it, not just on particular days when you allow it. What if you and Murdoch have to work through the evening one weekend, what are you going to do then? Loosen up mother, and get a life! You're not as free as you think, yet! Why do you keep on denying your feelings? You've got to take life as it comes."

And she was right, so the detective work needed to start all over again. For months and months I worried away at this conundrum so much so that I was sometimes mentally exhausted with the emotional stress, but I was determined to find the solution.

So why did I lack the confidence to eat and drink exactly what and whenever I wanted?

Well, the eating bit was fairly simple. That all went back to my grandmother and mother, and the way they compared me unfavourably with my sister Elsie, which resulted in my firm belief that people didn't like you, let alone love you, and you were ugly, unless you were thin. And so the thinner the better, I had thought. This belief had been ingrained in me for so long, it was only natural that I could only gradually loosen my grip. And gently build my confidence bit by bit.

Murdoch had always told me that it didn't matter to him what shape or size I was, but I'm not sure if I had ever really believed it. But around the time of my chat with Elaine, I did actually start to put on a few pounds, and guess what? It didn't put him off me at all.

He said there's nothing unattractive about someone who is above the average size – what is unattractive is the way some of them are self-conscious about it, and try to hide or disguise it, instead of being proud and dressing in clothes that suited and made the most of their figure. And it occurred to me that it wouldn't make one iota of difference to me what weight he was, so why should my size bother him?

But there was something still worrying me – my age. I was in my early fifties by then, and I was still wearing denim jackets and slim-fitting jeans. That in my head was youthful. I weighed eight and a half stone, and if I let go dieting completely, I was afraid of growing old, and looking fat and frumpy. And you know what happens when you grow old – you die. And an unconscious fear of death can prevent you from growing up.

I had to acknowledge this, and grow up myself now, accepting life on life's terms and the batterings I had given myself. When I had kicked against life, it just turned round and kicked me straight back even harder. But unlike my mother, I never gave up hope that I would find the answer. If I had given up, I would have become as depressed as she was, and been rushing towards death like her.

So steadily over the months, I just let go – I had taken the final step. Practice makes perfect, so they say, and soon I was enjoying eating what I fancied every day of the week, not just when we were having a drink.

At first it was marvellous going round the supermarket and enjoying all the smells of freshly baked bread, which previously I had not dared to breathe in, in case it proved too much of a temptation. Every day was a feast at the start, but now I'm more used to it, and not thinking about it all the time. I still appreciate eating what I like every day, although it has evened itself out, and it's more balanced now. Food is no longer my first waking thought in the morning – (' is this an eating day?'). The obsession has gone, and I'm free!

I believe that alcohol abuse, anorexia, and the abuse of prescribed drugs (the three problems which I feel qualified to talk about, because they are the ones which have affected my life) are all branches of the one tree.

The root causes and effects of each, however superficially different, are basically the same. People like myself are self-harmers, and it doesn't matter what you choose to use or abuse, it's *why* you do it in the first place.

They are all a kickback, if you like, against psychological neglect, physical, sexual or emotional abuse suffered in childhood or adolescence. Everybody's story will be different, but this is mine.

And in my case, everything stemmed from patterns of thinking and behaviour passed on from one generation to the next, like a family curse in Greek tragedy, and only stopped when I gained some understanding of the underlying causes.

Finding the solution to my eating problem led on to sorting out my drinking – they were so closely connected that they merged into each other. Benders were a thing of the past, but I was still strictly controlling it, rather than being able to enjoy it freely as people do who have never had an alcohol problem.

Obviously I didn't want the past to return. Equally, whilst I was enjoying having a drink, it isn't so enjoyable when you're consciously counting your drinks.

And drinking on a Saturday or Sunday evening whether I felt like it or not, and rigidly refusing to drink on any other night even if I did feel like it – well that was removing half the pleasure of drinking at all.

Drinking should be a spontaneous enjoyment, and I was resenting it becoming an ordered routine. It was like telling myself in advance how I was going to be feeling on certain days of the week, and that isn't freedom. Nobody's feelings are hidebound, they can change day by day, hour by hour, even minute by minute – they are mercurial.

So why was I exerting such tight control over my drinking at that time? It arose out of fear. And that led me to ask myself: "Why have I been frightened and anxious most of my life?"

And I realised that it had started in childhood. There had never been any certainty in my life – my parents and my grandmother were never consistent in their behaviour towards me.

Like the way I never knew whether I would get a glass of lemonade and a piece of cake or a verbal lashing from my grandmother, or how my father would react when he came home from work in the evening. Sometimes he seemed pleased to see me – on other occasions when I went up to greet him, he just didn't want to be bothered by my stories of the day. Even when he did, and I thought that I had done something that would please him, he would always find something to criticise. He always had a better idea about how things should be done. Nothing was ever quite good enough, which in turn gave me the feeling that *I* was not quite good enough. And when I made a mistake, he would say I was worse than useless.

My father's nature and traits were inherited from his mother. She was the most important influence in his life. Like her, he was more concerned with correctness than with humour and being natural. Un-questioningly he adopted her opinions and her attitudes as his own, and as far as they were both concerned, there was only one way to do things – and that was *their* way. "Don't do as I do – do as I tell you!" This saved him a lot of time and trouble trying to explain anything, but he didn't realise that saving this most precious time caused more problems than he would have cared to admit.

I have inherited his determination and strength of character, and that has served me well through life. But my troubles came when I took most of his opinions and attitudes, and adopted them as my own. No wonder I ended up with problems, and resulted in me being so mixed up, I didn't know who I was. In a similar way, my father had accepted his mother's opinions, thinking that was his true identity. He had never grown up to be independent of her, at least until she died, whereas I was always a rebel.

One example of how I always tried to be like my father, but often later regretted it, was my antique shop. Over the years my father had bought and sold antiques – this was something he enjoyed, and when he retired, he encouraged me to do the same, and suggested that I open a shop. So I did this to please him, but in less than a year I was fed up with this. I used all sorts of excuses – the shop wasn't doing too well, but this was because I really wasn't interested. It finally dawned on me that this just wasn't for me, and I was doing something that *he* had really wanted to do.

In any company, if anyone dared to disagree with him, especially about politics, he was unwilling to compromise, and his immediate response was to rise from his chair and tell my mother: "Go and get our coats. It's time that we were going."

My mother was more complex, though. Mainly she would be unpredictable if anyone upset her ordered routine, and as she got older this got worse and worse. Her relentless pursuit of cleanliness in the house meant that she could not be comfortable in it. She could only relax in other people's homes, where such extremes of perfection were not even thought about.

Like my mother, I was more sensitive than either my father, brother or sister, and I absorbed and took more seriously the contradictory ways in which the grown-ups in my family treated me, and was therefore more easily hurt.

They seemed not to be upset about what was to me confusing behaviour – I was, but would never have been allowed to say. Also I tried to hide this, as I did not want to upset my father, as he was the most important person in my life. And I had already seen my mother cry, and I would rather just be upset myself than hurt either of them again.

But I became so mixed up and frustrated that one of the things I did at school was to start to bite my nails. My mother would give me a row for this, and paint what was left of my nails with bitter aloes to try and stop me doing it again – treating the symptom, instead of finding out why I was doing it in the first place. This was the first time I can remember taking things out on myself, because I could not express what I was feeling to my parents.

I could also get rid of my frustrations by getting up to mischief at school. As I got older, alcohol gave me comparative social ease in situations where I didn't know people, and I could cover up my uncertainties and anxieties. I could become the joker, the comedian, the clown, a smile and a laugh masking the inner sadness.

And I know now why I always used to seek the limelight and try to be the centre of attention, especially at parties. It was because as a child I was made to feel small and unimportant. When I got older, I could only assert my importance with the help of a drink, but then my behaviour became over the top.

But gradually the sadness took over, and I felt as if I was in mourning most of the time. More than one person told me that I was the unhappiest looking person that they had ever seen. This bugged me so much that it led me to the realisation that my sadness was really suppressed anger. But not knowing the real cause, I couldn't blame anybody other than myself, which led to such a powerful pent-up frustration and emotional pain, that for me benders, however inappropriate, were the only release.

It was a big step for me to translate my newly discovered knowledge into action, and release my tight control of both my eating and drinking.

But I did it – over time. There's no overnight solution. It takes time to absorb the answers.

We had come so far, and were now rounding the final bend, and heading down the home straight.

Having gone back through my childhood, and fully come to terms with the negative influences that my family had had upon me, I could now confidently assert my right to be myself – the real self that I wanted to be, not the person that other people expected me to be. I now understood what previously I couldn't reach – the true *me*. Up until now I had been pulled in opposite directions, and so could never be free to be the master of my own life.

One half of me I had copied from my mother – her ways of doing things were my ways. The other half of me was devoted to pleasing my father. His opinions became my opinions, so obviously there was no room left for my individual personality. And that's why I had never known until now who I really was – my parents had never encouraged me to grow as a separate independent person. I was trying to find my true self, and hiding from myself at the same time. And if this wasn't enough, I was also hiding from the truth. I did know what was wrong, because I was the only one who had lived my life, but the things that had hurt me had been put to the back of my mind, although they were still troubling me.

All this had led me to feel a sense of unreality, that I was on the outside, looking in on life. The only thing I did know was that there was something wrong with me, but not knowing what it was only increased my sense of isolation. My mind was locked in a prison, and I couldn't find the key, even though I had searched everywhere round about me for it. At that time there was no light of understanding at all, and that is sheer purgatory, or hell on earth. It was my dark night of the soul.

And if you lace all these feelings with booze, the effect is devastating, it was as if I was dissolving or disappearing into a black hole, a place where there is no emotional pain. I've been told that when I was like this, I couldn't be reached. I suppose that for some people this is the point of no return, and only madness lies beyond. But I was lucky – after a long sleep I was always able to come back to reality.

But now that's all in the past. Now, the vacuum left inside me when I extracted the false personality created by me to please my family and everybody else could be filled with the person I really was, and wanted to be.

And once you are able confidently to assert your right to be exactly the person you want to be, then anything is possible.

Don't get me wrong. I'm not saying that suddenly overnight you can become a millionaire, a brain surgeon or a rock star. That sort of thing is entirely dependent upon your natural abilities, chance and other people in the outside world.

What I am saying is that, when you are at one with yourself, then within your own four walls (both the four walls of your own home, and the four walls of your new-found self) you can do anything. Certainly, in the case of the anorexic or so-called 'alcoholic' – these are just labels – you can eat or drink normally again. You can do what you want, and be what you want to be.

These sort of fundamental changes do not happen overnight. It's one thing to know the answers – quite another to take the time to absorb them. But the more I did it, the easier it became. Each day I took a hen's stride forward. Now I have built up my confidence, and no longer count either my drinks or my calories. Murdoch and I are not drinking any more than we did before alcohol became a problem – in fact sometimes we drink a little bit less. And I'm not exactly gorging myself with food either.

But the point is that we don't worry about it, and just eat and drink what we want and when we want.

We don't worry about money any more either – we can take life as it comes. And actually it's coming along not too badly. Murdoch started doing some freelance journalism, which was a bit more lucrative than our previous work.

Because of his previous radio and television experience, he had written to the *Ayrshire Post*, our local newspaper, suggesting that he could contribute a weekly family finance column. We had received no reply, and had almost forgotten all about it. Then, about a year later, we received a telephone call out of the blue saying that they were interested.

Murdoch was invited to go along to their offices to meet the Editor Tommy Workman and Jim Cuthbert, the Business Editor, and was offered his first real break – the chance to write a regular column in the paper as he had suggested. This soon led to the editorship of a Scottish recruitment newspaper, and now most recently he has started up his own public relations consultancy.

Elaine believes that we have both succeeded in sorting our problems out, and often spends the evening with us, when her crowded social schedule allows. And my son John and I are back on friendly terms again. So everyone's happier, with a lot to look forward to.

Hopefully reading my story will prompt other people to make similar discoveries about their own lives, and have the strength and courage to make the changes they want.

Obviously, not everyone who has had problems in childhood turns to booze. It might be food, pills, gambling or whatever when your behaviour is out of control. You don't have to be hurting yourself physically – it can be emotional damage that you are causing, to yourself and other people, or damage to your reputation. But I know now that there is no such thing as alcoholism, or any of these other so-called addictions. What we are all really addicted to is our own learned behaviour (or misbehaviour), and anyone who persists in believing otherwise has got it wrong.

Today Murdoch and I are free, and are able to take a drink (or not) as and when we wish. We are in the real world now.

So for us, alcoholism isn't an illness or a disease. Neither is it a chemical imbalance, a faulty gene, a defective chromosome, or any of the other descriptions that I've heard at *AA* meetings. That's why nobody has ever come up with a cure. Alcoholism is a self-harming behaviour problem, which can be corrected.

Once you see it, it's so simple. It's as plain as the nose on your face what's wrong. But, like your nose, when you're so close to the problem, it's actually extremely difficult to see.

For me, understanding is everything. Once I understood, and took the time to realise and fully absorb how ridiculous my behaviour had been, how and why would I ever want to go back to it? That wouldn't be me at all. Especially as now I have got peace of mind, and that's all that I had ever wanted. The best thing that anyone can have in this life is peace of mind, and the freedom to live your life in the way that you want to. I have found freedom from the voices of the past that had been so powerful in shaping the false image I had of myself, and found the confidence to see myself in a completely new light and to truly believe what I saw.

The main purpose of writing this book has been to try to help the many other people who are suffering from so-called addictions, and who like us have found it difficult in this modern day and age to accept the 12-step programme, but who, up until now, have felt that there was no other way.

We have proved that there is.

AA was formed in 1935, which is (at the time of writing) exactly 70 years ago. It is now time they acknowledged that, after their allotted life span of three score years and ten, it is now time for them to move over and allow progress in this field to resume.

And for anyone who still thinks that you cannot make a responsible drinker out of an alcoholic, there is an old Chinese proverb which goes: 'Those who say it cannot be done, should not interrupt the person doing it.'

Unlike in *AA*, where everybody is kept down by being told to believe in their own powerlessness, we want to empower people to believe that through discovery, and with the right support, they too can overcome their unnecessary mental suffering, and like the newly crowned King Henry V in Shakespeare's play, face the world and say: 'Presume not I am the thing I was!'

Appendix One
The Twelve Steps

Sweet soul, take heed of perjury.

*William Shakespeare, **Othello***

MANY people who praise *AA's* 12-step programme have probably never read it. We therefore have decided to include them at the end of this book, so that readers can judge for themselves whether they have any relevance whatsoever to recovery from a self-harming behaviour problem, or whether they are just the creed of a quasi-religious cult.

1.   We admitted we were powerless over alcohol, that our lives had become unmanageable.

On the surface, this first step seems quite reasonable. But nobody is powerless to change their behaviour and regain control of their life. Our story proves that it is possible to learn the coping skills for life that were previously lacking. It was this lack of coping skills when we were growing up that had made our lives unmanageable, not alcohol. Alcohol had just made things worse.

2.   Came to believe that a Power greater than ourselves could restore us to sanity.

3.   Made a decision to turn our will and our lives over to the care of God as we understood Him.

AA always says that it is not a religious organisation, but the second and third steps seem to belie this. It is non-denominational, but it is certainly religious. If you want to join a religious organisation, that's fine, but we believe that it is more responsible to take control of your own life. There's nobody more powerful than you are to change your own life.

4. Made a searching and fearless moral inventory of ourselves.

5. Admitted to God, to ourselves, and to another human being the exact nature of our wrongs.

6. Were entirely ready to have God remove all these defects of character.

7. Humbly asked Him to remove our shortcomings.

8. Made a list of all persons we had harmed, and became willing to make amends to them all.

9. Made direct amends to such people wherever possible, except when to do so would injure them or others.

10. Continued to take personal inventory and when we were wrong promptly admitted it.

It is obviously true that most alcoholics will have physically or emotionally hurt at least one other person during the course of their uncontrolled drinking. Making restitution might make you feel better, but to make this the basis of a 'recovery programme' from an illness/disease is surely to miss the point. We were the ones who have been hurt somewhere along the way just as much as any-one else. Your treatment of other people, however regrettable, was a symptom of how much you had been hurt yourself.

11. Sought through prayer and meditation to improve our conscious contact with God as we understood Him, praying

only for knowledge of His will for us and the power to carry that out.

12. Having had a spiritual awakening as the result of these steps, we tried to carry this message to alcoholics, and to practise these principles in all our affairs.

Back to religion again. For us, getting in touch with our real selves and finding our true identity was the key. We both believe that there's a god, but not one that wants to do everything for you. You've got to find your own way in this life.

Appendix Two
Destroying the Myths of Alcoholics Anonymous

Men are most apt to believe what they least understand.

Montaigne, **Essays**

AT the same time as we were spending all those weeks and months in Cambridge, trying to trace the causes of our present problems back to their roots in childhood and adolescence, we were also continuing to go to *AA* meetings in order to work out why it was that we found their ideas so unacceptable, and their teaching so ineffective in aiding our recovery.

Gradually, as we talked together late into many a long night, a picture began to form and become clear in our minds. We began to see and to understand how, as a result of coincidence and misunderstanding, various unrelated and irrelevant ideas united, and then coalesced into the philosophy of the early members of *AA*.

These ideas, although a strange mixture of contemporary medical ignorance and evangelical Christianity, at least reflected the current thinking of the time in these two fields. However, instead of changing, developing and progressing over the years, this philosophy became fixed, to the extent that barely a dot or a comma was allowed to be changed in the *AA* bible, the so-called *Big Book*, as it moved from one edition to the next.

Because this book has become the basic text for our Society and has helped such large numbers of alcoholic men and women to recovery,   there exists a sentiment against any radical changes being made in it.

Big Book, Preface, p.xi
(all page numbers in this Appendix refer to the 3rd edition of the *Big Book*).

It is boasted that the *AA* programme for recovery has not changed one iota since it was first formulated. It is indeed true that it has remained perfectly preserved, as if in formaldehyde, for seventy years. But whether this is an achievement of which to boast, we must beg leave to question. What *AA* seems to forget is, that for something to remain perfectly preserved, it has first to be dead.

This would have been a matter of no great importance if *AA* had remained a small self-help group comprising a few non-proselytising individuals.

Unfortunately, it has been allowed to grow into the worldwide cult that we know today. Ideas which would have proved harmless in a small group, have, when promulgated by an international organisation that has been accorded a near monopoly in the field of alcoholism treatment, served only to virtually halt any progress or advancement of knowledge and understanding being made in that field since 1935, not to mention unnecessarily denying countless hundreds of thousands of sufferers from alcoholism the opportunity of making a real, genuine, or what we call a *radical* recovery.

Let us just try to imagine the difficult situation faced by people back in the 1930s, who were concerned in any way, and for what ever reason, with the apparently problematical epidemic of alcoholism.

Judging by their contributions to, and their remarks quoted in the *Big Book*, contemporary medical practitioners were baffled, and were compelled to fall back on the concept of alcoholism as a mysterious and deadly disease, which was basically physical, but which also in some inexplicable way involved the mind as well.

I met a kind doctor who explained that though certainly selfish and foolish, I had been seriously ill, bodily and mentally.

Big Book p.7

Dr William D Silkworth expressed it in this way:

The body of the alcoholic is quite as abnormal as his mind.

Big Book, The Doctor's Opinion, p. xxiv

He then goes on to develop his idea of alcoholism as some kind of allergy, which just does not make sense in terms of any dictionary definition, or common understanding of the meaning of the word.

...the action of alcohol on these chronic alcoholics is a manifestation of an allergy; that the phenomenon of craving is limited to this class, and never occurs in the average temperate drinker.

Big Book, The Doctor's Opinion, p. xxvi

The misconceptions and ignorance about the true nature of alcoholism are understandable and forgivable, given the limited new knowledge generally available at that time. Ideas about alcoholism had not changed or progressed substantially since ancient times – certainly in 1935 nobody in the general public domain had come forward with any markedly different theories. The trouble is, however, that this lack of true understanding forms the very foundations upon which the whole edifice of *AA* philosophy has been constructed, and because these foundations have never been reinforced in the light of new knowledge and understanding, the whole building should now be pronounced unsafe, demolished and built entirely anew.

Again and again, as if the writers are attempting to convince them-selves more than the reader, the *Big Book* dogmatically asserts that there is no cure for this 'disease'. The constant repetition suggests a desperation to quash any possible dissent, and betrays the vacuum at the heart of the discourse, left by the absence of any logical argument or of any reasonable proof.

We have seen the truth demonstrated again and again: 'once an al-coholic, always an alcoholic'.

Big Book p. 33

We know that no real alcoholic ever recovers control.

ibid p.30

We are like men who have lost their legs; they never grow new ones. Neither does there appear to be any kind of treatment which will make alcoholics of our kind like other men. We have tried every im-aginable remedy. In some instances there has been brief recovery, followed always by a still worse relapse.

ibid pp.30/31

Just occasionally there is a brief glimpse of a more flexible mind at work, a mere suggestion that what is being said may not remain cast iron forever:

Physicians who are familiar with alcoholism agree there is no such thing as making a normal drinker out of an alcoholic. Science may one day accomplish this, but it hasn't done so yet.

ibid p.31

In all probability, we shall never be able to touch more than a fair fraction of the alcohol problem in all its ramifications. Upon therapy for the alcoholic himself, we surely have no monopoly.

ibid Foreword p.xxi

Only for the dogmatic, declamatory, tub-thumping tone to return, all too soon:

The delusion that we are like other people, or presently may be, has to be smashed.

ibid p.30

We suspect that, consciously or unconsciously, this inflamed rhetoric is designed and intended to camouflage an inner core of uncertainty, even ignorance. For the truth is that the founders of *AA* were no more aware of the real radical causes of alcoholism than their successors are today. But they seek to disguise this void with an outward show of bravado and seemingly confident certainty.

Occasionally however the mask slips, and momentarily their vulnerability, their quintessential lack of true understanding, is allowed to show.

Speaking about the puzzling behaviour of an alcoholic on a bender, Bill Wilson says:

Why does he behave like this? If hundreds of experiences have shown him that one drink means another debacle with all its attendant suffering and humiliation, why is it that he takes that one drink? Why can't he stay on the water wagon? What has become of the common sense and will power that he still sometimes displays with respect to other matters?

Perhaps there never will be a full answer to these questions. Opinions vary considerably as to why the alcoholic reacts differently from normal people. We are not sure why, once a certain point is reached, little can be done for him. We cannot answer the riddle.

ibid p.22

Once in a while he may tell the truth. And the truth, strange to say, is usually that he has no more idea why he took that first drink than you have. Some drinkers have excuses with which they are satisfied part of the time. But in their hearts they really do not know why they do it. Once this malady has a real hold, they are a baffled lot. There is the obsession that somehow, someday, they will beat the game. But they often suspect they are down for the count.

ibid p.23

It is to fill this vacuum of ignorance at the core of the *AA* philosophy that the 'God thing' was brought in, for the so-called 'programme for recovery' is in fact nothing more nor less than the basic precepts of the Oxford Group, an inter-denominational Christian fellowship which was at the peak of its popularity at the time of *AA*'s formation in 1935.

Bill Wilson first came into contact with the Oxford Group when Ebby, one of his former drinking companions, but then newly converted to Christianity and sobriety, came to visit Wilson prior to the latter's last period of hospitalisation for alcoholism.

Ebby explained to Wilson the Oxford Group philosophy which had enabled him to overcome his drinking problem.

First, he said, he had surrendered his life to God, having recognised that he could not run it himself. Then he tried to be honest with himself, making amends whenever possible to people he had hurt. Next he tried to give himself up completely to the service of others. Finally, although he had not previously believed in the power of prayer, he found to his surprise that now it worked for him.

It is surely not co-incidental that Ebby's account of his new-found beliefs reads suspiciously like *The Twelve Steps* that Bill Wilson was afterwards to formulate for *AA*.

There is a further coincidence that we find difficult to swallow, and that is concerning Wilson's 'spiritual experience' which preceded and apparently led to his conversion to sobriety.

It has been suggested that this experience may have been spirituous rather than spiritual - in other words the sort of hallucinatory semi-dream that one can have whilst withdrawing from a heavy intake of alcohol, and has not been uncommon in our own experience. What happened to Wilson has also been put down to the after-effects of the medication (probably belladonna) that would have been used on him during his period of hospitalisation. Our own theory is more prosaic. It is that his "spiritual experience" was more a result of the power of suggestion.

The *Big Book* describes how:

A certain American businessman...had floundered from one sanatorium to another. He had consulted the best-known American psychiatrists. Then he had gone to Europe, placing himself in the care of a celebrated physician (the psychiatrist, Dr Jung) who prescribed for him.

The doctor said, "You have the mind of a chronic alcoholic. I have never seen one single case recover, where that state of mind existed to the extent that it does in you."

Our friend felt as though the gates of hell had closed on him with a clang.

He said to the doctor, "Is there no exception?"

"Yes," replied the doctor, "there is. Exceptions to cases such as yours have been occurring since early times. Here and there, once

in a while, alcoholics have had what are called vital spiritual experiences."

Jung had (apparently) suggested that, in order for an alcoholic to have any hope of recovery, he must first have a spiritual experience, so lo and behold, Bill Wilson amazingly and coincidentally, immediately goes and has one. It is described as follows in the *Big Book*:

There was a sense of victory, followed by such a peace and serenity as I had never known. There was utter confidence. I felt lifted up, as though the great clean wind of a mountain top blew through and through. God comes to most men gradually, but His impact on me was sudden and profound.

ibid p.14

By the time we get to the chapter "There Is a Solution", it is suggested that all the early members of *AA* had had such an experience, and that to do so, in fact is a prerequisite for recovery from alcohol.

The great fact is just this, and nothing less: That we have had deep and effective spiritual experiences which have revolutionised our whole attitude toward life, toward our fellows and toward God's universe. The central fact of our lives today is the absolute certainty that our Creator has entered into our hearts, and lives in a way which is indeed miraculous. He has commenced to accomplish those things for us which we could never do by ourselves.

***ibid*.** p.25

But Wilson had rushed in where angels feared to tread, he had gone too far too quickly for his own followers to accept. Acting on a suggestion (which he had misunderstood) that he must have a spiritual experience, he duly and obligingly had one.

He then generalised from that, and issued a blanket prescription that all alcoholics who wished to recover must have one also. The *AA* membership of the time must have felt sufficiently uncomfortable about this to make their misgivings known, for by the time of the printing of the second edition of the *Big Book*, a special appendix had to be added, which is as near to a retraction as we have ever heard from *AA*:

The terms 'spiritual experience' and 'spiritual awakening' are used many times in this book, which, upon careful reading, shows that the personality change sufficient to bring about recovery from alcoholism has manifested itself among us in many different forms.

Yet it is true that our first printing gave many readers the impression that these personality changes, or religious experiences, must be in the nature of sudden and spectacular upheavals. Happily for everyone, this conclusion is erroneous.

In the first few chapters a number of sudden revolutionary changes are described. Though it was not our intention to create such an impression, many alcoholics have nevertheless concluded that in order to recover they must acquire an immediate and overwhelming 'God-consciousness' followed at once by a vast change in feeling and outlook.

Among our rapidly growing membership of thousands of alcoholics such transformations, though frequent, are by no means the rule.

ibid p.569

Unfortunately, Wilson's interpretation of the full meaning and implications of Jung's advice is, we believe, erroneous. He failed to report quite accurately all of what Jung actually said, (it is not revealed, but we assume that the patient was Wilson himself,) whilst extracting two words only which he could utilise as suitable for his own purposes.

Our reading of Jung's words have convinced us that what he is really saying is, not that the alcoholic must have a sudden blinding vision of 'God-consciousness' which will miraculously convert him into a saint on earth. The spiritual experience he is describing is more akin to the deliberate and painstaking self-analysis which we found ourselves undertaking on our road to radical recovery. It is more an inward mental journey, lit only by the lamp of one's own gradually increasing stock of self-understanding and wisdom, rather than a brilliant floodlight from some external source peremptorily shone upon oneself like a thunderbolt from the blue.

Jung's suggested course of action for the alcoholic seems in retrospect to be very similar to our own method of examining how attitudes, motivations, and perceptions of ourselves which we had inherited from our own childhood and adolescence had become not only outworn and obsolescent, but also positively detrimental and even destructive to the continuation of an effectively functioning everyday life, and certainly to our chances of future contentment and happiness.

The full text of what Jung is supposed to have said, as reported in the *Big Book*, runs as follows:

He said to the doctor, "Is there no exception?"

"Yes," replied the doctor, "there is. Exceptions to cases such as yours have been occurring since early times. Here and there, once in a while, alcoholics have had what are called vital spiritual experiences. To me these occurrences are phenomena. They appear to be in the nature of huge emotional displacements and rearrangements. Ideas, emotions, and attitudes which were once the guiding forces of the lives of these men are suddenly cast to one side, and a completely new set of conceptions and motives begin to dominate them. In fact, I have been trying to produce some such emotional rearrangement within you. With many individuals the methods which I employed are successful, but I have never been successful with an alcoholic of your description.

ibid p.27

Jung here is indicating the direction of the road to recovery as we understand it. Where he is mistaken, however, (assuming that his conversation has been accurately reported) is in thinking that it is possible to "produce" a recovery in anyone, let alone a chronic alcoholic. We believe that it is only possible to point out the route – it is entirely up to the other person whether or not he or she follows it. That is what we are trying to do in this book. We describe the long and weary road that we took, and leave a map to guide all those who take the same track after us, in the hope that they will find the going easier than we did, for knowing where it leads.

So far we have seen how *AA* came into being as a result of a historically accidental and coincidental conjunction of two elements:

1. the contemporary medical orthodoxy of the time

2. the combination of a fundamental misunderstanding of Jung's advice, together with the coincidence of both the *AA* founders being familiar with the evangelical doctrine of the Oxford Group, Wilson through his meeting once again his former drinking partner Ebby, and Dr Bob through his own membership of the group. These factors ensured that *AA* would be a powerfully quasi-religious organisation, however much it chooses to deny or disguise the fact.

Mix 1. and 2. together in a large bowl, stir well, and you have an instant recipe of a proselytising group of would be do-gooders, preaching the gospel of life-long sobriety to the world of alcoholics, laced with a generous dash of hellfire and brimstone to keep the unruly masses in a state of quiescent obedience.

Frankly, the whole thing is a total nonsense. What it all boils down to in essence is that they are saying that alcoholism is a progressive, incurable and fatal illness or disease of mind and body. That's the bad news, right? But the good news is that you can get continuing remission on a daily basis, by turning your life and your will over to the care of God (as you understand Him), confessing your sins, making amends for them, and living the rest of your life in accordance with His will (not yours) and carrying the message to others.

If all this were true, sufferers from all manner of other incurable ill-nesses, AIDS, cancer, motor neurone disease, what have you, would be knocking on *AA*'s doors, begging to share their secret. But they're not, of course, and why? Because it simply is not true. The *AA* programme for recovery from alcoholism is no such thing. It is merely a means of cauterising or suppressing the symptoms, with an outward show of so-called spirituality thrown in for good measure. Once you admit that you are an alcoholic, then that's your label for life giving you a new false identity. The person behind the label who should really matter remains anonymous, and never gets treated.

However, none of this would be of the slightest significance or im-portance, if *AA* had remained a small localised group with no further plans for expansion. Had it done so, it would have died out long since, as its quaint collection of ideas came to be recognised as such, and the medical, scientific and psychiatric professions would have been forced to dig deeper, research more thoroughly, in order to discover more pro-gressive, more realistic, and more radical solutions.

But the ambition of one man, Bill Wilson, caused *AA* to become a worldwide organisation, and to assume and be accorded a monopolistic position in the field of alcoholism treatment. (The other cofounder, Dr Bob, by contrast, was quite content to remain at his post in the City Hospital, Akron, Ohio, spreading the *AA* message to individual alco-holics who came to him as patients.)

Wilson's nature and personality traits come over very strongly and clearly as he tells his own story in the *Big Book*:

I fancied myself a leader, for had not the men of my battery given me a special token of appreciation? My talent for leadership, I imagined, would place me at the head of vast enterprises, which I would man-age with the utmost assurance.

ibid p.1

I'd prove to the world I was important.

ibid p.2
Though my drinking was not yet continuous, it disturbed my wife. We had long talks when I would still her forebodings by telling her that men of genius conceived their best projects when drunk; that the most majestic constructions of philosophic thought were so derived.

ibid p.2

Business and financial leaders were my heroes.

ibid p.2

For the next few years fortune threw money and applause my way. I had arrived. My judgement and ideas were followed by many to the tune of paper millions.

ibid. p.2

When these fantasies failed to materialise, he recast them in a different mould, and satisfied his ambitions by throwing himself into a new role as the cult leader of the *AA* movement, whilst Dr Bob contented himself with beavering away on a humbler, but more practical level.

People will probably ask us, "What exactly do you have against *AA*? Haven't they done a great deal of good?"

Our answer would be, yes – and no.

Yes, in that, at the time, back in 1935, there was not very much else available.

And yes, in that they have got a few million alcoholics sober, who might otherwise have been either drunk or dead.

But no, emphatically *no*, inasmuch as they have effectively stalled any real progress that might have been made in the treatment of alcoholism for the past seventy odd years. One of the reasons is that in their traditions they put 'principles before personalities' which means that they have no respect for individual people coming up with new ideas. They have assumed a monopoly on the whole subject, and the rest of the world, including the media and many doctors, has quietly acquiesced.

In the case of the latter, it is hardly surprising, as it has obviously suited them to do so. Here was a group of patients, with whom since time immemorial they had made little progress, suddenly taking over responsibility for their own treatment, setting up their own psychiatric wards (because that's what *AA* meetings are like) and, at the same time, not asking for, and even refusing to accept any funding for doing so. Little wonder that doctors all over the world have tacitly agreed to keep quiet, and just let them get on with it.

Money comes into it as well. Private clinics have sprung up over the years using the *AA* programme, charging patients a typical £3000 /£3500 per week. A lot of these patients are not private, but referred and paid for by the NHS, which means the individual taxpayer. This contravenes one of the *AA* traditions which states that 12-step work is never to be paid for. And all this nonsense from apparently trustworthy organisations who come complete with celebrity endorsements.

We should be looking into the question of who is training all these so-called counsellors. As far as we know, anyone can call themselves a counsellor.

Where and when we criticise *AA*, we do so more in sorrow than in anger. We believe that if they had only been less dogmatic and inflexible in their outlook, had they been more open and receptive to new ideas, new thinking, new ways of looking at things, then the movement could have become a potent force for innovation, change and progress in the field of understanding and treating alcoholism. Had they not been so hidebound by their own unchangeable dogma, then the discoveries that we have made, at the expense of so much time, effort and pain, would undoubtedly have already been made many years ago.

Occasionally, here and there in the *Big Book*, one comes across the odd few phrases which suggest a more open-minded attitude, a possible willingness to accept the possibility of change, but they are too fleeting and infrequent.

But in most fields our generation has witnessed complete liberation of our thinking. Show any longshoreman a Sunday supplement describing a proposal to explore the moon by means of a rocket and he will say, "I bet they do it - maybe not so long either." Is not our age characterised by the ease with which we discard old ideas for new, by the complete readiness with which we throw away the theory or gadget which does not work for something new which does?

We had to ask ourselves why we shouldn't apply to our human problems this same readiness to change our point of view.

ibid p.52

One paragraph even seems to be describing our own hopefully rational approach, in which we first analyse, and then discard the *AA* philosophy, before moving on to construct one of our own which is more soundly based in the ground rock of our personal experience.

Logic is great stuff. We liked it. We still like it. It is not by chance we were given the power to reason, to examine the evidence of our senses, and to draw conclusions. That is one of man's magnificent attributes. We...would not feel satisfied with a proposal which does not lend itself to reasonable approach and interpretation.

ibid p.53

AA claims a membership of several million alcoholics, all dedicated to the task of solving their common problem, alcoholism. Were they not constricted by the straitjacket of their inherited philosophy, the fellowship could have been the largest and the most powerful medical research organisation ever known to man. Even at this late stage, it still could be. If only they were prepared to consider the possibility of new ideas, different from those to which they have traditionally adhered. Their absolute refusal to change is their greatest weakness.

We do not claim to make the final word on the subject, only to have carried the torch first lit by Bill Wilson and Dr Bob one stage further along the way. Others will no doubt take over where we leave off, and so progress will continue to be made, until full and complete knowledge and understanding is reached. We will merely add a few final words from the *Big Book*, which seem a singularly apt way in which to describe what we have tried to do.

We can only clear the ground a bit. If our testimony helps sweep away prejudice, enables you to think honestly, encourages you to search diligently within yourself, then, if you wish, you can join us on the Broad Highway. With this attitude you cannot fail. The consciousness of your belief is sure to come to you.

ibid p.55

Appendix Three
Alcoholics can be cured – despite AA
by
Dr Arthur H. Cain

I am the voice of one crying in the wilderness.

The Bible, John 1:23.

THIS article first appeared in the *Saturday Evening Post* on 19 September 1964, but is still relevant today. What is tragic is that nothing seems to have changed since.

From the *Saturday Evening Post* 19 September 1964

ALCOHOLICS <u>CAN</u> BE CURED – DESPITE AA
By Dr Arthur H. Cain

An expert charges that Alcoholics Anonymous has become a dogmatic cult that blocks medical progress and hampers many members' lives.

It is time we made a thorough investigation of Alcoholics Anonymous in the interest of our public health. *AA* is identified in the public mind as a God-fearing fellowship of 350,000 'arrested alcoholics' who keep one another sober and rescue others from the horrors of alcoholism. Unfortunately, *AA* has become a dogmatic cult whose chapters too often turn sobriety into slavery to *AA* Because of its narrow outlook, Alcoholics Anonymous prevents thousands from ever being cured. Moreover *AA* has retarded scientific research into one of America's most serious health problems.

My own experience with *AA* began in 1947. As a psychologist and investigator into the causes and cure of uncontrolled drinking, I have attended about 500 *AA* meetings in over 40 states and a dozen foreign countries. At first I was tremendously impressed with *AA*'s altruistic efforts on alcoholics' behalf. Its members would perform prodigies of selfless service, no matter what the hour, by meeting the helpless and sodden in hospitals, flophouses and homes, and offering their sympathy, a helping hand, and their own example that temptation could be withstood. At the weekly meetings, which all *AA* members attended, there was a true sense of humility and a devout belief in God (We 'came to believe that a Power greater than ourselves could restore us to sanity') and the fellowship of man – the original tenets of *AA*. New members were given the freedom to question *AA*'s guiding principles codified in the Twelve Traditions and the Twelve Steps of Recovery.

Over the years a disturbing change began to take place. As an increasing number of alcoholics joined *AA* chapters, many turned out to be misfits who had rejected Christianity, Judaism or the Kiwanis Club. Dogmatic and opinionated in their non-beliefs, they found in *AA* an instrument for a new kind of bigotry. Their only meaning in life was that they had heroically become 'arrested' alcoholics. Arrogant egoists, they soon dominated many of *AA*'s 10,000 chapters. Weekly meetings, once spontaneous and exciting, became formalized and ritualistic. Anyone who questioned *AA*'s principles or even expressed curiosity, was handed the slogan 'Utilise, Don't Analyse', and told to sit down. The desire to help others degenerated. As one disheartened former *AA* member told me: "I felt nobody cared what happened to Mary W. I felt they were just interested in another alcoholic who would become another notch in their belts. I felt as if I was being pressed into serving their cause and building up their oligarchy."

With this growing dogmatism came a Dark Ages attitude toward any scientist who might differ with official *AA* doctrine. According to the *AA* litany, alcoholism is a physical disease which can never be cured: 'Once an alcoholic, always an alcoholic.' The corollary is: 'A reformed alcoholic must live *AA* from day to day and never leave *AA*.'

Actually, there is no scientific evidence that alcoholism is an incurable, physical disease. According to current evidence, the origin of uncontrolled drinking is psychological. A person drinks to ease anxiety, depression, boredom, guilt, timidity, inarticulateness. An alcoholic *learns* to become one; he is not born that way. This means that many alcoholics can return to normal drinking without fear of ending up on Skid Row. Over the past 17 years I have treated more than 50 alcoholics who no longer need to attend meetings or receive treatment. Most important, over 20 of my patients have learned to drink normally, to use alcohol as a beverage, not a psychological crutch.

Yet when scientists have reported similar findings, *AA* members have often set out to discredit them. In 1957 Doctors Melvin L. Selzer and William Holloway of the University of Michigan came up with the then startling report that 13 confirmed alcoholics had become social drinkers. Because of the pressure of an influential *AA* member, the state agency that provided the funds for the study virtually ordered the two scientists to omit what it called these 'embarrassing' findings. Doctor Selzer published his findings anyway.

In 1962 Dr D.L. Davies, after a study at Maudsley Hospital in London, declared that seven men who had been alcoholics were able to drink normally after treatment, some had been drinking without problems for as long as 11 years. Doctor Davies concluded that 'the generally accepted view that no alcohol addict can ever again drink normally should be modified'. Some *AA* members branded the scientist's report 'immoral, because it might cause some members to drink'.

Dr E. M. Jellinek, a cofounder of the Yale School of Alcohol Studies and a dean of researchers in the field of alcoholism until his death in 1963, was drawing on his own experience when he declared: "Alcoholics Anonymous have naturally created the picture of alcoholism in their own image…and there is every reason why the student of alcoholism should emancipate himself from accepting this exclusiveness as propounded by *AA*."

Not only has *AA* interfered with scientific investigations, it has pre-vented medical and psychological treatment which runs counter to its own theories. At one New York City hospital, for instance, the physi-cians preferred using paraldehyde to treat acute intoxication. But then *AA* members implied that they would stop referring patients there if paraldehyde was used. The doctors were persuaded to switch to anoth-er drug, chloral hydrate. As the physician in charge of the alcoholics' ward explained, the *AA* non-scientists had discovered that paraldehyde was a form of alcohol. Actually, chloral hydrate is the more toxic drug. In fact, its indiscriminate use in another New York hospital has left some patients more intoxicated upon discharge than when they were admitted.

While *AA* adherents battle scientific inquiry that does not fit *AA*'s narrow theories, its chapters often attempt to assume control of mem-bers' lives. Purporting to offer everything needed for human fulfilment, the fellowship now boasts of a 'ladies' auxiliary', called Al-Anon, for spouses of members and even a division for members' children called Alateen. It suggests that the youngsters open their meetings by reciting this incantation: "We will always be grateful to Alateen for giving us a Way of Life and a wonderful, healthy programme to live by and en-joy!" Implied is the distressing theory that there is no other way of life for alcoholics except that of *AA* – a life in which every waking hour is devoted to the struggle for sobriety.

The wife of a Texas member described some unfortunate conse-quences of *AA*'s creed that the struggle against alcohol must be the most important ambition in a member's life. "This must be placed above wives or husbands, children, homes or jobs. They must be ready to abandon these things at any time. The tragic part is, some of them while searching for this sobriety and serenity actually do exactly that." How pervasive the obsession with *AA* can become was poignantly demonstrated by a patient who had come to me because of worries about her *AA* husband. He had proposed that they move their bed into the *AA* clubhouse so they might be 'available 24 hours a day, just in case an alcoholic wandered in'.

For many members, of course, staying sober is a fierce challenge daily. But under the *AA* programme, the lives of many are so sterile that their growth as human beings is hindered. Taught to rely on slogans and compulsive *AA* routine, some are unable to face the fact that they are alcoholics because they are psychologically sick. It is for this reason that many *AA* members never recover.

A New Hampshire novelist and former *AA* member, who has been continuously sober for eight years, described this human waste when he wrote to me: "I have met members who are actually afraid to think. They have made a high fence of *AA*, which shuts them out from all pleasurable and vital aspects of life."

Behind the *AA* fence, the original principle that alcoholics must be humble before God has been turned into the dictum that alcoholics are God's chosen people. This theme is preached in meetings and through books and pamphlets. A typical illustration is a booklet titled *Around the Clock With AA*, published recently by an *AA* group in California. One passage declares: "God in His wisdom selected this group of men and women to be the purveyors of His goodness... He went right to the drunkard, the so-called weakling of the world. Well might He have said to us: 'Unto your weak and feeble hands I have entrusted power beyond estimate. To you has been given that which has been denied the most learned of your fellows. Not to scientists or statesmen, not to wives or mothers, not even to my priests or ministers have I given this gift of helping other alcoholics which I entrust to you.'" Such idolatry causes the believer to see himself as all knowing, and turns the missionary into the zealot.

AA's creeds not only infect its own members, but also pervade public education. Most of what we hear or read about alcoholism is inspired by *AA* adherents spouting *AA* dogmas. City, state and private agencies frequently fill all key posts with *AA* members. One western state actually requires that personnel assigned to its alcoholism programme be *AA* members for at least two years. No professional experience is needed. The *AA* philosophy also dominates the National Council on Alcoholism, the only nationwide public-information agency on alcoholism. *NCA*, which is supported by public donations, has over 60 affiliated information committees scattered throughout the country. Although both *NCA* and *AA* deny that they are officially connected, many members of *NCA*'s staff and some directors are *AA* members. *AA* members serve as directors in eight out of ten *NCA* information centres in the largest cities in the United States.

Thus, it is not surprising that *NCA* continues to parrot the *AA* line that alcoholism is a 'progressive disease for which there is no known cure, but which can only be arrested'. Further, *NCA* in a series of radio and TV commercials actually stated that the American Medical Association had declared alcoholism to be a disease, although the *AMA* has restricted itself to general statements that the alcoholic is 'sick'. Time and again, I have heard public figures recite *AA–NCA* myths and propaganda as if they were gospel.

I once heard Arthur Flemming, former Secretary of Health, Education and Welfare, read verbatim a pronouncement on alcoholism which I knew had been prepared a year earlier by *NCA*'s public relations firm. Flemming offered the now familiar statistic' that there are five million alcoholics in the United States. This figure is based on a study Doctor Jellinek of Yale conducted 18 years ago in a small community; he thought he had found that three per cent of the population were alcoholics. *NCA* applied this percentage to the whole nation. Doctor Jellinek, a great physiologist but no statistician, repudiated his own formula in 1956. The five-million figure is only a guess, for no scientific count of alcoholics has ever been made.

While *NCA* issues well-intended but sometimes questionable facts and theories, *AA* officials, when pressed, often hide behind the famous Tenth Tradition, which states that "Alcoholics Anonymous has no opinion on outside issues, hence the *AA* name ought never be drawn into public controversy." This device enables members of *AA* to make outrageous assertions which *AA*'s headquarters promptly disavows when challenged. "Many people I have tried to help," said one Chicago member, "have abandoned the programme just because they couldn't take the *ex cathedra* homilies on drugs, alcohol, psychiatry, medicine, sociology, biology, to name a few subjects on which they speak with authority."

Much of *AA*'s failure can be blamed upon a lack of forward-looking, constructive leadership. Writer Jerome Ellison recently spent several months as a paid consultant to *AA* evaluating the fellowship's publications and activities. At national headquarters in New York City, Ellison declared, committee politics took up half the working day, and gossip was venomous. Everybody was an expert, Ellison went on, "with a cluster of ideas closed to amendment." He related how one member had submitted to the *AA* monthly bulletin an article which showed that nearly all southern and a great many northern *AA* chapters were racially segregated, and that *AA* had failed to keep pace with the growing, problem of Negro alcoholism. The article was turned down on the ground that it "might disrupt *AA* unity".

Ellison's most damning indictment concerned the rule made by *AA*'s non-alcoholic board of trustees that no change can be made in *AA*'s theories on alcoholism, even though they are nearly a quarter of a century old. "Despite the fact that the rank and file teems with exciting, relevant, informed and up-to-the-minute experience," Ellison declared, "none of it is permitted to appear in book form. To publish such literature, it is felt, would be to risk heresy."

Needless to say, I do not suggest that *AA* be abolished or that a single member quit. That *AA* helps many thousands stay sober is obvious. But Alcoholics Anonymous should return to its original purpose of being a much-needed first-aid station. The 'arrest' of uncontrolled drinking is the essential first step in becoming a recovered or cured alcoholic. During this critical period, the alcoholic needs the sympathy and understanding that only another alcoholic can give. But after three months or so, when the shakes have subsided and the cobwebs are beginning to clear, the recovering alcoholic should go ahead. He should not be taught that he must remain forever crippled and bound by the paralysing concept 'Once an alcoholic, always an alcoholic'. It is at this point that the patient needs a different kind of understanding: an objective, dispassionate, clinical understanding that physicians, psychologists and pastoral counsellors, not *AA* members, are trained to give. Only after he has undergone a rigorous and lengthy revision of his personality should he attempt to drink normally again, and then only if he desires to do so.

After all, sobriety in itself is not a way of life. It is simply the absence of intoxication. It is what one does with his sobriety and his life that is important.

Our Love Story

When Murdoch and I first got together, we were told that our relationship would never last, and some people actually tried to separate us. But I love Murdoch as much today as I did the day I married him. We have gone from strength to strength in all aspects of our lives.

'On this couple drop a blessed crown.'

*William Shakespeare, **The Tempest.***

Conclusion

Alcoholism is not a progressive, incurable disease or illness which alcoholics are born with. It is a behaviour problem, a response to dysfunctional childhood.

Alcoholics are not addicted to alcohol. They are addicted to the escape that alcohol affords. Escape from life, or certain aspects of life which they find too difficult or too painful to cope with, or the associated feelings that go with not coping. Alcohol is a quick fix, and addiction means an habitual response.

Alcoholics are commonly told they are "powerless over alcohol" and that there is therefore nothing they can do about it but accept lifelong abstinence. But we have proved that the opposite is true, and that there's a lot that alcoholics can do for themselves.

If, as we did, alcoholics choose to identify and address their issues from the past, or alternatively, simply take a more mature attitude of responsibility for their behaviour and learn to deal with life, most will be able to drink responsibly once again if and when they so wish.

We hope this book will have been of some help to people affected by alcohol, and it comes with our sincere best wishes for the future.

Contacts

You can contact Lilian and Murdoch either via their website:

www.alcoholicscandrinksafelyagain.com

or by e-mail at **lilianandmurdoch@aol.com**

For more information on this and other titles please contact the publishers via their website:

www.melrosebooks.com

About the Authors

Lilian MacDonald was born in Lochwinnoch, Renfrewshire, Scotland in 1943, where she and her brother and sister spent their childhood. Her grandparents had a smallholding where they worked as market gardeners.

As an adult, in spite of her alcoholism and eating disorder, Lilian has worked successfully in several varied spheres, most notably owning and managing a country inn in South Ayrshire.

Lilian married Murdoch in 1993, and has two children from a previous marriage, John and Elaine.

***

Murdoch MacDonald was born in Putney, London in 1946. After graduating from Magdalene College, Cambridge, he first worked in banking, and then public relations.

He wrote a regular column in a prestige Scottish business magazine, hosted and produced a weekly radio programme and took part in a television series, both about family finance.

Since Lilian and he resolved their alcohol problem, Murdoch now writes for the business page of three local newspapers in Ayrshire, and in addition runs his own PR business.

He also has two children from a previous marriage, Kirsty and Grant.